DISCARD

ENVIRONMENTAL DISASTERS

The *Exxon Valdez* Oil Spill

Elspeth Leacock

002000277451

Facts On File, Inc.

The *Exxon Valdez* Oil Spill

Facts On File, Inc.
132 West 31st Street
New York NY 10001

For Library of Congress Cataloging-in-Publication Data information, please contact Facts On File, Inc.
ISBN 0-8160-5754-0

Facts On File books are available at special discounts when purchased in bulk quantities for businesses, associations, institutions, or sales promotions. Please call our Special Sales Department in New York at (212) 967-8800 or (800) 322-8755.

You can find Facts On File on the World Wide Web at
http://www.factsonfile.com

A Creative Media Applications, Inc. Production
Writer: Elspeth Leacock
Design and Production: Alan Barnett, Inc.
Editor: Matt Levine
Copy Editor: Laurie Lieb
Proofreader: Tania Bissell
Indexer: Nara Wood
Associated Press Photo Researcher: Yvette Reyes
Consultant: Thomas A. Birkland, Nelson A. Rockefeller College of Public Affairs
    and Policy, University at Albany, State University of New York

Printed in the United States of America

VB PKG   10 9 8 7 6 5 4 3 2 1

This book is printed on acid-free paper.

Contents

Preface

This book is about the devastating *Exxon Valdez* oil spill, which took place off the coast of Valdez, Alaska, in 1989. That year, just after midnight on March 24, the supertanker *Exxon Valdez* ran aground on a reef in Prince William Sound. The rocky reef tore open the hull of the tanker, spilling millions of gallons of Alaskan crude oil into the sound.

Almost everyone is curious about such catastrophic events. An interest in these disasters, as shown by the decision to read this book, is the first step on a fascinating path toward learning how disasters occur, why they are feared, and what can be done to prevent them from hurting people, as well as their homes and businesses.

The word *disaster* comes from the Latin for "bad star." Thousands of years ago, people believed that certain alignments of the stars influenced events on Earth, including natural disasters. Today, natural disasters are sometimes called "acts of God" because no human made them happen. Scientists now know that earthquakes, hurricanes, and volcanic eruptions occur because of natural processes that the scientists can explain much better than they could even a few years ago.

An event is usually called a disaster only if it hurts people. For example, an earthquake occurred along Alaska's Denali fault in 2002. Although this earthquake had a magnitude of 7.9, it killed no one and did little serious damage. But a "smaller" earthquake—with a magnitude below 7.0—in Kobe, Japan, in 1995 did billions of dollars in damage and killed about 5,100 people. This quake was considered a disaster.

A disaster may also damage animals and the environment. The *Exxon Valdez* oil spill in Alaska is considered a disaster because it injured and killed hundreds of birds, otters, deer, and other animals. The spill also killed thousands of fish—which

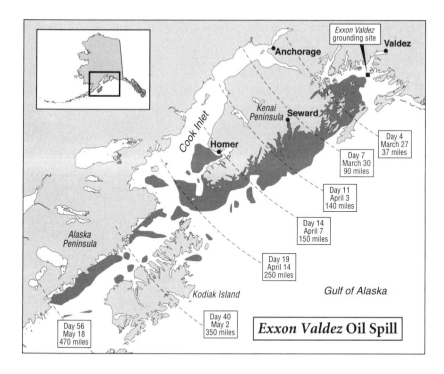

This map shows how the oil spread along the Alaskan coast in the weeks following the spill.

many Alaskan fishers rely on to earn their livelihoods—and polluted the places where the fish spawn.

Disasters are also more likely to happen when people make decisions that leave them *vulnerable* to catastrophe. For example, a beachside community is more vulnerable to a hurricane than a community that is inland from the ocean. When people choose where to live, they are also choosing what sort of natural disasters they may experience in the future; they are choosing the sort of risks they are willing to take. People who live on beaches in Florida know that hurricanes may damage or destroy their houses; people who live in certain areas of California know that earthquakes may strike at any time.

The things that people do to make themselves safer from less dangerous natural events, like heavy rains, sometimes actually make the people more vulnerable to bigger disasters. For example, when a dam is built on a river to protect people downstream from floods, the dam may prevent small floods that would otherwise happen once every 25 years. But when a really big storm occurs—the kind that comes once every 100 years—the dam may not be able to hold back the water. Then a surge of water that is even bigger than it would have been without the dam will come rushing down the river and completely destroy all the buildings in the area.

At first, it may seem easy to blame human disasters, like the *Exxon Valdez* spill, on one or a few people. Some observers blame the spill on the captain, who was responsible for the ship. But perhaps the spill was another crewmember's fault. Maybe the blame should fall on Exxon, because that corporation owned the ship. Or maybe all Americans are to blame, because the United States uses a lot of oil for heating houses and driving cars. Finding the "right people" to blame can be difficult. Is it anyone's fault that people suffer from natural disasters? Natural disasters at first appear to be merely unfortunate "acts of God."

This book and the other books in this series will demonstrate that mistakes people made before a disaster often made the disaster worse than it should have been. But they will also show how many people work to lessen the damage caused by disasters. Firefighters, sailors, and police officers, for example, work very hard right after disasters to rescue people, limit additional damage, and help people get back to their normal lives. Behind the scenes are engineers, architects, legislators, scientists, and other citizens working to design new buildings, make new rules about how and where to build buildings, and enforce those rules so that fewer people will have to risk their lives due to disasters.

The books in this series will show what can be done to reduce the chances that people and communities will suffer from natural and human disasters. Everyone has a role to play in making communities safer. The books in this series can show readers how to become part of a growing movement of citizens and experts that can help everyone make good decisions about disasters.

Please note: All metric conversions in this book are approximate.

Introduction

Environmental disasters often leave many layers of problems in their paths. After the immediate danger and damage to the environment, people may only gradually realize how that damage will affect the lives of human beings. A disaster caused by human error is usually followed by resentment, anger, and finger-pointing over who is to blame and, ultimately, who is responsible for financial losses. Depending on the size of the disaster, it may be unclear who will repair the damage and how that will be accomplished. A major disaster, however, can also lead to beneficial changes. People may join together, combine their resources, and learn how to avoid this type of trouble in the future.

When a petroleum product is accidentally or intentionally released into the environment as a result of human activity, the result is called an oil spill. Spills can emanate from tankers, *pipeline* breaks, trucks, trains, and even oil wells. They can happen when people are manufacturing, transporting, or drilling for oil. Most oil spills are environmental accidents that occur in deep ocean waters, far away from residential areas. Scientists know little about these spills' immediate or long-term damage to the environment because the oil eventually sinks to a depth in the ocean at which scientists are unable to investigate.

Oil spills from tankers account for most of the world's largest oil spills. Tankers are the best way to transport large volumes of oil. Oil spills near populated areas are human-made environmental disasters that cause harm and destruction in many ways. An oil spill spreads quickly and can be influenced by weather conditions and water currents. Without speedy attention, oil spills can wreak havoc on a community for generations to come.

Launching pollutants into our air, land, and water can damage the health of human beings, plants, and animals. Cleanup

The Argo Merchant tanker ship ran aground and broke apart off Nantucket Island, Massachusetts, in high winds and 10-foot (3-m) seas. The tanker spilled over 7 million gallons (26.5 million l) of fuel oil into the water. (Photo courtesy of National Oceanic and Atmospheric Administration)

crews may become sick from breathing in oil fumes. Animals may become trapped in pools of oil that have polluted their habitat. Oil gets trapped in the animals' fur, destroying their ability to maintain body temperature. Birds can no longer fly when their feathers are drenched in sticky oil, and they become sick from eating clams or mussels that have been soaked in sludge. Plants are unable to grow in sand and soil that have been poisoned by oil.

The economic impact resulting from oil spills and their cleanup can touch people near and far from the actual disaster. Poisoned or declining fish populations can ruin regions where people rely on fishing for their livelihood. Shore towns that count on tourism for revenue can go bankrupt when their beaches are covered in oil. The way of life of a community where a disaster occurs is sometimes disrupted forever.

Oil spills may also become a political issue when people realize how spills may affect big business, hamper the nation's ability to acquire this precious resource, and lead to new laws regarding energy consumption. Consumers may feel the results when prices for gas or home heating fuel rise, forcing them to make adjustments in their personal budgets.

The United States uses approximately 25 percent of the world's oil. More people, bigger cars, larger homes, more travel, and higher demand for heating and air-conditioning are just some of the reasons the United States wants to find new places to drill for oil.

The Trans-Alaska Pipeline carries oil from Alaska's North Slope *oil fields* to Valdez Harbor. The plan to construct the pipeline, completed in 1977, had been met with fierce opposition. Local residents, environmentalists, and politicians fought for years over the safety of such a project and the effect it would have on the pristine landscape of the region. The story of the *Exxon Valdez* oil spill in Alaska's Prince William *Sound* made real the fears of these people. After leaving the Port of Valdez, this *supertanker* was responsible for the largest oil spill in U.S. history. The disaster and its aftermath reveal how an accident resulting from human error, inadequate resources, and natural obstacles can lead to the irreparable destruction of an *ecosystem* and its inhabitants and of traditions that had existed for hundreds of years.

After the *Exxon Valdez* disaster, government and business leaders realized how inadequately prepared they were to deal with such a catastrophe. In 1990 the Oil Pollution Act (OPA) passed by Congress outlined a much stronger set of rules for preventing and responding to oil spills. Unfortunately for the people of Prince William Sound, that measure came too late to protect their precious way of life.

In *The* Exxon Valdez *Oil Spill,* you will learn exactly how this disaster occurred; what human and natural elements contributed to the damage; what progress was made day by day by the thousands of people who flocked to the region to help; what great costs have been paid as a result of the nation's need for fuel; and what steps have been taken to make sure that such a disaster never happens again. The book also includes a photo essay illustrating how marine life can recover from an oil spill, a time line, a chronology of catastrophic oil spills, a glossary, and a list of books and web sites for further study and review.

Please note: Glossary words are in italics the first time that they appear in the text. Other words defined in the text may also be in italics.

CHAPTER 1

Supertankers and Spills

At one time, there were no supertankers (huge ships for carrying oil and other liquids) and no *crude oil* (oil that has not yet been processed into usable products like gasoline) in Prince William Sound. Valdez, a small village that rests on this large arm of water reaching inland from the Gulf of Alaska, was populated with people who depended on the abundant marine life found in the sound for their living.

In 1977 the Port of Valdez became the terminal, or end, of the Trans-Alaska Pipeline System, and since that year, the community has mostly depended on oil. The oil travels through a pipe 48

An aerial view of the coastline along the Valdez arm located between Prince Willliam Sound and the harbor of Valdez, Alaska. When the port became a terminal for the Trans-Alaska Pipeline, the town's character as a small fishing village was drastically altered. (Photo courtesy of Phil Schermeister/ CORBIS)

inches (122 cm) in diameter 800 miles (1,290 km) across Alaska, from the oil-rich North Slope to Valdez Harbor, the northern-most ice-free port in the United States.

With the building of the pipeline, some local people feared that an oil spill was likely to happen and warned of the risks. By the spring of 1989, however, about 9,000 tankers had loaded up with oil in Valdez and left safely for *oil refineries* in other Pacific ports in California, Washington, and Hawaii. There had been a few close calls and small spills, but North Slope oil brought jobs and a lot of money to Alaska, and the United States needed oil. The rewards outweighed the risk of an oil spill, and over time, more and more oil passed through Prince William Sound.

Supertankers

The pride of Exxon's fleet, the Exxon Valdez *had successfully navigated many ocean voyages carrying oil before the disaster of March 24, 1989. (Photo courtesy of Associated Press)*

In 1989 Exxon was the nation's biggest oil company, and the *Exxon Valdez* was the pride of its fleet of tankers. The ship cost $125 million to build. Only three years old, it was the newest and best-equipped ship in the fleet. At 987 feet (301 m), it was longer than three football fields, making it one of the largest ships in the

world. Standing on end, the ship would tower as high as most skyscrapers.

The *Exxon Valdez* was a supertanker. These extremely large ships hold large tanks in their hulls for carrying oil or other liquids and have a capacity of over 100,000 tons (91,000 mt). (The hull is the main frame of the ship.) Supertankers that have a capacity between 100,000 and 500,000 tons (91,000 and 454,000 mt) are called *Very Large Crude Carriers* (VLCCs). Ships that can carry over 500,000 tons (454,000 mt) are called *Ultra Large Crude Carriers* (ULCCs). (The *Exxon Valdez* was a VLCC. It's carrying capacity is discussed further in the sidebar "A Very Large Crude Carrier" to the right.) A supertanker is highly automated, and the control room, or *bridge*—packed with consoles, computers, radar screens, radio equipment, a depth finder, rudder indicators, and a long-range navigation device—is the brain of the ship. The bridge and crew facilities are at the back, or *stern*, of the ship.

On March 23, 1989, when the *Exxon Valdez* set out from Prince William Sound, it was carrying 53 million gallons (201.5 million l) of crude oil and proceeding at a speed of approximately 13 miles (21 km) per hour. A supertanker's top speed is about 15 miles (24 km) per hour. This may not seem very fast when compared to the speed of a car on land, but a supertanker has a huge mass. Therefore, when it travels with any velocity at all, its momentum is very large. Fully loaded and at top speed, a supertanker takes 3 miles (4.8 km) to come to a stop. In an emergency, a tanker moving "full ahead" must be thrown into "full reverse" to come to a stop as quickly as possible. This procedure, called a *crash stop*, can take 10 to 14 minutes.

A Very Large Crude Carrier

The *Exxon Valdez* could carry 1,484,829 barrels of oil—but just how much oil is that? There are 42 gallons (159 l) in a barrel of oil. That means that the *Exxon Valdez* could carry more than 62 million gallons (235 million l) of oil! An average classroom is around 20 feet (6.1 m) long, 20 feet wide, and 8 feet (2.4 m) high. To fill such a classroom with oil, 25,091 gallons (94,944 l) would be needed. Therefore, the oil carried by the *Exxon Valdez* would fill 2,485 classrooms right up to the ceilings!

Oil Spills around the World

The *Exxon Valdez* disaster was the worst oil spill in U.S. history, but there have been other, worse spills. The largest oil spill of all time was the result of war. During the Persian Gulf War in 1991, Iraqi forces set fire to more than 600 oil wells in Kuwait. The wells continued to burn as much as 6 million barrels of oil a day for over eight months, putting millions of tons of pollutants into the air. The Iraqis blasted pipelines and storage tanks and emptied loaded tankers, deliberately spilling as much as 420 million gallons (1590 million l) of crude oil into the Persian Gulf. That is over 38 times the 11 million gallons (41.6 million l) spilled by the *Exxon Valdez*.

Offshore oil rigs have caused some of the world's largest spills. For example, on June 3, 1979, the Ixtoc-1 oil well blew, spilling about 140 million gallons (530 million l) of crude oil into the waters of the Gulf of Mexico.

On June 3, 1979, an offshore oil rig called Ixtoc-1 off the coast of Mexico blew out, eventually spilling 140 million gallons (530 million l) of crude oil into ocean waters before it was brought under control the following year. (Photo courtesy of National Oceanic and Atmospheric Administration)

There have been many tanker spills greater than the spill by the *Exxon Valdez.* Since tankers ply the waters of every sea, there are few shores in the world that are not potentially threatened by tanker accidents. Large tankers have run aground, sunk, caught fire, crashed into other ships, and broken apart in storm waves, spilling oil into every major body of water and oiling the shores of every continent. In March 1978, the *Amoco Cadiz* sank off the coast of France, spilling over 68 million gallons (257 million l) of oil. In July 1979, almost 43 million gallons (163 million l) of oil were spilled in the Caribbean when the *Atlantic Empress* collided with another ship. The year 1983 saw the world's largest tanker spill on August 6, when the *Castillo de Bellver* lost 78.5 million gallons (297 million l) off South Africa. The *Haven* spilled 42 million gallons (159 million l) in the Mediterranean port of Genoa, Italy, in April 1991. In February 1996, the *Sea Empress* ran aground off the coast of Wales, spilling over 21 million gallons (79 million l).

Although there have been many greater tanker spills than that of the *Exxon Valdez,* few have been as damaging to the environment. In November 1988, for example, the *Odyssey* spilled almost four times as much oil, but the spill was in deep water in the Atlantic Ocean, far from any shorelines. The oil spilled from the *Exxon Valdez* into Prince William Sound entered a much smaller and shallower body of water, and the resulting *oil slick* was close to the shore. The damage to the environment was far greater from the smaller spill than from the larger one. The sidebar "The Biggest Spill of All" on this page has more on oil pollution.

The Biggest Spill of All

Tanker spills are among the most destructive forms of oil pollution, but tanker spills are not the greatest sources of such pollution. The greatest source of oil pollution is not accidents or oil well blowouts or even acts of war—it is storm drains! If people pour their old oil down storm drains in the street when they change the oil in their cars, it eventually reaches the ocean. This oil, combined with runoff from roads and industrial and municipal waste, adds up to an average of 363 million gallons (1.4 billion l) of oil a year draining into the ocean. The *Exxon Valdez* spilled 11 million gallons (41.6 million l).

The *Exxon Valdez* Leaves Port

On Thursday, March 23, 1989, at about 9:30 P.M. Alaska Standard Time (AKST), the *Exxon Valdez* left the Port of Valdez. From the bridge of the ship, Captain Joseph Hazelwood could see the tanker stretched out hundreds of feet before him. As a captain known for his intelligence and skill, Hazelwood knew the waters of Prince William Sound well.

Standing in the large, dimly lit control room with the captain was Ed Murphy, the harbor pilot. Murphy's job was to steer the *Exxon Valdez* through the maze of islands, shoals, and *reefs* in the sound and out into open water. He understood the local weather and water currents and knew which conditions might endanger the vessel. James Kunkel, the chief mate, was also there, but he was tired. As chief mate, Kunkel was in charge of docking and loading the ship while it was at the terminal. Under his watch, water had been carefully pumped out of the ballast tanks of the *Exxon Valdez* as $50 million worth of crude oil was pumped into the cargo tanks in its hold. The hold was divided into 16 cargo tanks that could hold a total of 1,484,829 barrels or 211,000 tons (191,420 mt) of oil. That made the supertanker a VLCC.

As the pilot steered the great ship out of the harbor, Captain Hazelwood went below to his cabin. According to regulations, he should have remained on deck with the pilot, but Hazelwood and Murphy had been on this route many times before. The captain knew that his ship was in good hands, and he had paperwork to do. The ship's 2,800-horsepower engine propelled the giant tanker through the water at about 11 knots—a speed close to 13 miles (21 km) per hour.

At 9:50 P.M. (AKST), Third Mate Gregory Cousins relieved a grateful Chief Mate Kunkel. Exhausted, Kunkel went straight to bed in his cabin below. As the ship neared the Valdez Narrows, it entered fog. The narrows is a bottleneck with a great rock that juts out of the water right in the middle of the channel. Called Middle

Thirteen days after the Exxon Valdez ran aground in Prince William Sound, a tugboat pulled the supertanker off Bligh Reef and into port. (Photo courtesy of Bettmann/CORBIS)

Rock, it also has the ominous nickname of "the Can Opener." One harbor pilot describing the job said, "We all know what the stakes are. You've always got to be on your toes. I see these ships as eggs that are a quarter of a mile long. You can't make mistakes with them." However, the *Valdez* passed the dangerous rock safely, and the fog began to lift. With open water ahead, it was time for the pilot to return to the Port of Valdez. His job was done. The captain returned to the control room to take over command of the ship as Murphy climbed down the side of the tanker to the pilot boat bobbing in the water below and departed for the shore.

The radar screen showed a lot of ice ahead. Hazelwood could not tell from the radar whether the chunks of ice were harmless—the size of a car, for example—or big, dangerous pieces larger than a house. Large pieces of ice called "growlers" could rip open the hull of the ship. To avoid the ice, Hazelwood decided to go around it.

There are two shipping lanes in Prince William Sound—one for incoming tankers, and the other for outgoing ones. This traffic separation plan keeps the tankers in Prince William Sound in deep water during their passage, with a required distance of 0.5 miles (0.8 km) between them. When small icebergs sometimes drift into the shipping lanes, a captain has the choice to slow down his ship to push through them without harm, or—traffic permitting—change shipping lanes.

Hazelwood gave orders to the *helmsman*—the person who was steering the tanker—to turn the vessel left, leaving the outgoing shipping lane. Before leaving his lane, the captain radioed the U.S. Coast Guard. After checking their radar screens, members of the Coast Guard told Hazelwood that there were no other ships nearby and that it was okay for the *Exxon Valdez* to cross lanes. The time was near midnight.

CHAPTER 2

Collision

Captain Hazelwood told Third Mate Cousins to order the ship back into its own shipping lane in a little while. He went over this order a few times to be sure that Cousins knew exactly what to do. Then the captain left the control room again and went to his cabin. This was against regulations, but he wanted to finish up his paperwork.

After a few minutes had passed, Third Mate Cousins gave the order to turn toward the right—but something had gone terribly wrong. The huge tanker had crossed the incoming lane and was headed toward rocky Bligh Reef. The ship began turning back, but it was too late. A supertanker needs a long time and a lot of space

In the port of Valdez, Alaska, hundreds of tankers are loaded up with oil each year, supporting the nation's ever-increasing need for oil. (Photo courtesy of CORBIS)

On April 9, 1989, 16 days after the Exxon Valdez *hit a rocky reef in Prince William Sound, oil swirls can be seen on the surface of the water near Naked Island. (Photo courtesy of Associated Press)*

to turn, and the *Exxon Valdez* had run out of both. Cousins phoned the captain and said, "I think we're in serious trouble." The ship had not made a significant enough turn. Then there was a terrible lurching as the tanker plowed into the rocky reef, tearing gashes in its light metal hull and ripping open eight of its 16 oil storage tanks. Thick, black crude oil gushed out from the tanks with such force that it created a wave 3 feet (0.9 m) high. The time was 12:04 A.M. (AKST) on Friday, March 24.

Below, in his cabin, Kunkel awoke with a start. Later, he said, "The vessel began to shudder and I heard a clang, clang, clang. I feared for my life. I thought I would never see my wife again. I knew my world would never be the same."

The captain bounded up a stairway to the control room and immediately took command of the floundering tanker. He ordered officers to wake up the crew below and to ready the lifeboats and rescue gear. He also began a series of orders to stabilize the tanker, because it was beginning to list, or lean, to one side. As oil poured out, there was a real danger that the great hull would break under the tremendous stress of its own weight. If the tanker broke up, the crew would not survive in the frigid water or toxic oil that surrounded the vessel.

The captain sent Kunkel to the cargo control room to see how badly the ship was damaged. The gauges were hard to read because there was so much movement in some of the tanks. Oil was pouring out fast. Kunkel found that the tanker had already lost about 100,000 barrels. This meant that in less than half an hour, over 4 million gallons (15 million l) of thick, black crude oil had entered the pristine ecosystem of Prince William Sound. As the minutes turned to hours, oil continued to gush out at an alarming rate. Three hours later, the gauges indicated another 2 million gallons (7.6 million l) had been dumped into the icy waters. All around the tanker, the oil fumes became so strong that some of the crew feared they would pass out from breathing them. Kunkel was afraid that he "would not live to see the sun rise."

Drinking and Driving

At the time of the accident, two things were known about Captain Hazelwood. The first was that he was a highly skilled captain—one of the best. The second was that he was known to have had problems with alcohol in the past. Exxon knew that Hazelwood had been arrested several times for drinking and driving, but he had been treated for alcohol abuse at a clinic, and the company gave him another chance.

After the *Exxon Valdez* accident, Hazelwood told the Coast Guard that he had consumed two beers that day. But witnesses testified that they had seen him drinking two or three vodkas in a Valdez bar called the Pipeline Club. During his trial, much was said about Hazelwood's drinking on the day of the accident. Crewmembers testified that they had noticed the smell of alcohol on his breath, but they also said that he did not appear intoxicated in any way. In the end, the prosecution could not prove that the captain caused the wreck or that he was drunk at the time.

At 12:26 A.M. (AKST), the captain radioed the Valdez Traffic Center (VTC). "We've fetched up, run aground north of Goose Island, around Bligh Reef," he said, "and evidently, we're leaking some oil." His words would soon be seen as an outrageous understatement. Further discussion of Captain Hazelwood can be found in the "Drinking and Driving" sidebar above.

Oil and Water

By sunrise on Friday, March 24, 1989, the oil spilling from the *Exxon Valdez* was fast creating the largest oil tanker spill in the history of the United States. The ship did not break up or capsize, however, and there was hope that the oil slick could be contained and even cleaned up. That hope was based on two important facts: oil and water do not mix, at least not right away; and oil is lighter than water, so it rises to the surface of the water. With the right equipment, oil can be contained and then skimmed from the water, but this process must be started right away.

As soon as oil enters water, it begins to *weather*. The oil does not disappear; instead, it breaks down into its chemical parts and enters the environment in different ways. The lightest parts of crude oil evaporate in the first hours or days after a spill. Molecules that evaporate become part of the atmosphere. Some of the crew felt that they were going to pass out from the fumes on the night of the wreck because they were breathing in the evaporating oil molecules. At the same time, other molecules become part of the water in a process called *dissolution*. After *evaporation* and dissolution, the oil left on the water becomes heavier and stickier.

If the remaining oil is not scooped up immediately, rough seas will whip the oil with water. This causes the oil slick to form a floating pudding-like mess called *mousse*. Because mousse is 70 to 80 percent water, 100 barrels of oil can grow into 500 barrels of mousse. Mousse completely coats everything that it touches—beaches, birds, *otters,* seals, seaweed—and it is deadly. Creatures that become coated with this toxic goo usually pay with their lives. Oil may seep into their skin, affecting their internal organs. Birds cannot fly when their wings are weighed down with oil. Other mammals may hurt themselves while trying to remove oil from their eyes, nose, and mouth. To protect the water of Prince William Sound and all the living things that depended on that water, the cleanup had to begin before the oil turned to mousse and before it reached the shorelines. Unfortunately, this did not happen.

Alyeska's Responsibility

When the Trans-Alaska Pipeline was built, the state of Alaska created an official plan in case of an oil spill. The state's plan made the *Alyeska* Pipeline Service Company responsible for all spills involving pipeline oil. Alyeska was not a state or government agency, but a *consortium,* or partnership, of oil companies that built, owned, and operated the pipeline and terminal facilities. Exxon was just one of those companies. The names Alyeska and Alaska are from the same Native American word. In the Aleut language, the word *alyeska* means "mainland." Alyeska's origins are related in the "Alyeska and the Pipeline" sidebar on page 15.

According to the plan, Alyeska was to have ready at all times a trained response team, cleanup equipment, and boats to transport the team and equipment to the site of a spill within five hours of being called. In 1981, however, Alyeska began cutting its budget. Soon, its response team was no longer on duty 24 hours a day. As a result, employees with other jobs in the company were to be called in the event of a spill. Alyeska officials received the call regarding the *Exxon Valdez* just minutes after Captain Hazelwood made his call to the VTC at 12:26 A.M. (AKST).

Dan Lawn—an official from Alaska's Department of Environmental Conservation—and a Coast Guard official arrived

This picture shows a section of the 800-mile (1,280-km) Trans-Alaska Pipeline, which carries Alaskan North Slope crude oil from Prudhoe Bay south to Valdez, where it is transported out on supertankers. (Photo courtesy of Associated Press)

Alyeska and the Pipeline

When the Trans-Alaska Pipeline was built, it was the biggest private construction project in history. The pipeline was also one of the most expensive construction projects ever, costing over $8 billion. To accomplish this task, seven oil companies—Exxon, ARCO, BP, Hess, Mobil, Phillips, and Union—combined their resources to study, plan, design, and construct what would become one of the largest pipeline systems in the world. The new company that they formed was named the Alyeska Pipeline Service Company.

Alyeska hired 70,000 men and women to build the pipeline. Construction workers often labored 12 hours a day, seven days a week, in brutal conditions. Temperatures could reach −60°F (−51°C) during the dark winter months. The pipeline had to be built above ground for nearly 420 miles (676 km) to cross the frozen, treeless tundra. The pipe had to climb and descend three major mountain ranges and cross 800 rivers and streams. In all, the pipeline took two years and three months to build.

at the leaking tanker by speedboat around 3:00 A.M. (AKST). What Lawn saw in the dark horrified him. Around the tanker, the sea's surface was "a boiling cauldron. The oil was rolling up, boiling up, like it was cooking." Lawn watched for the lights of the cleanup crew's boat until, frustrated, he called Alyeska, using the tanker's radiophone. "What's going on? This ship is still leaking. You need to send out every piece of equipment you've got right away!"

Alyeska reassured Lawn that the equipment was on its way—but it was not. The equipment was buried in a warehouse. Worse, the barge for bringing the equipment out on the sound was not even in the water. The barge was in dry dock for repairs.

Exxon Gets Involved

Meanwhile, thousands of miles away in Houston, Texas, a phone rang. When Frank Iarossi answered the phone and learned of the disaster, he sprang into action. As president of Exxon Shipping Company, his first concern was for the ship, its cargo, and its crew. He ordered another tanker, the *Exxon Baton Rouge*, to head for the *Exxon Valdez*. The 42 million gallons (159 million l) of oil remaining on the *Valdez* would be transferred to the *Baton Rouge* in a process called *lightering*.

At 5:00 A.M. (AKST) Friday, as the first hint of light appeared in the eastern sky, 39 workers arrived at Alyeska's Valdez office. This was the response team that was supposed to be at the site of the spill within five hours. Those five hours had already passed as they began searching the warehouse for the equipment needed—large *skimmers* and deep-sea *booms*. Booms are long, flexible plastic tubes used to contain the oil, and skimmer boats are like ocean-going vacuums that suck the oil up. Once the equipment was located, an operator used a forklift to pick it up and carry it to the barge, which was back in the water by this time. At the harbor, another operator was supposed to lift the equipment onto the barge with a crane—but for hours there was only one operator to handle both jobs! As an observer explained, "The operator would snag containers of boom with the forklift, drive to the barge, climb into the crane to swing each container onto the deck, jump from the crane to the forklift, and speed back to the warehouse for another pickup."

As the sky grew light, Dan Lawn was still looking out from the tanker for signs of the response team. Later, he would say, "They told me they were coming, that they had all the stuff coming, that they'd be right out there. And we waited, and we waited, and we waited, and we waited."

Friday was a beautiful day—the air was warm, and the seas were calm—but with each hour that passed, the situation worsened. The oil slick was now 3 miles (4.8 km) long and 2 miles (3.2 km) wide, meaning that it covered an area of 6 square miles (15.5 km²), and it was growing larger all the time. Above it, a toxic blue haze of fumes hung in the air. On board the tanker, the fumes became so thick that some feared the ship might explode.

Compounding the crisis was confusion about who was in charge. Alyeska officials thought that they were responsible for the cleanup. Their plan, which had been approved by the state, was to corral the oil and use skimmers to scoop it up. This approach, using machines to clean up a spill, is a mechanical solution. But officials at Exxon Shipping thought that the spill was far too large to be cleaned mechanically. They thought that Exxon Shipping should take charge, and the company had its own plans. Also, the state of Alaska and the Coast Guard were involved in many of the decisions because it was their job to protect citizens and property.

Alongside the Exxon Valdez *sits a smaller ship, the* Exxon Baton Rouge. *The* Baton Rouge *successfully off-loaded crude oil from the* Valdez *in a lightering operation that eventually saved four-fifths of the oil carried by the* Valdez. *(Photo courtesy of Associated Press)*

This confusion caused time-consuming problems from the very beginning. For example, when Alyeska's barge was finally loaded with the skimmers and booms that its plans required, Exxon Shipping called to say that it urgently needed lightering equipment in order to transfer the oil remaining on the *Valdez* to the *Baton Rouge*. Therefore, many of the booms and skimmers had to be taken off the barge to make room, and the lightering equipment had to be loaded. When the barge finally reached the *Exxon Valdez*, almost 13 critical hours had passed. By this time, the oil slick had stretched out to 4 miles (6.4 km) long.

Lightering Begins

The difficult operation of lightering was eventually successful. When the *Baton Rouge* arrived, Captain William Deppe boarded the *Valdez*. He relieved Captain Hazelwood of his command and warned him, "This is something much bigger than you can imagine while sitting out here. Prepare yourself for a lot of attention when you get to shore." Hazelwood's life would never return to what it had been just the day before.

Captain Deppe's first concern was to save the crew, the ship, and its cargo. He later said,

> We were sitting there with our survival suits, life jackets, and very little information about what the bottom of the ship looked like. We didn't know whether she'd make it through the night. We certainly wanted to get as much oil off as possible, but our first consideration was all the people on board, making sure that we had an emergency response plan in case the ship did break in half or did start to capsize if she slid off the reef.

On Friday evening, as the first day of the oil spill turned to night, the slick now covered 18 square miles (46.6 km²). (The relative size of the spill at this point is discussed in the "How Big?"

How Big?

How big is 18 square miles (46.6 km²)? Think about a football field, which is 120 yards (110 m) long including the end zones, and 53 yards (48 m) wide. That makes it 6,360 square yards (5,280 m²). Imagine an area that big covered in thick, crude oil. Now imagine over 8,766 football fields covered in oil. That is how big the oil slick was by Friday evening.

sidebar above.) The process of transferring oil from one tanker to the other began early Saturday morning. The *Exxon Valdez* and the smaller *Exxon Baton Rouge* were rafted, or bound, together. As oil was pumped from the *Valdez* into tanks on the *Baton Rouge*, ballast water had to be pumped back in the *Valdez*'s tanks or the ship would collapse. The *Baton Rouge*—and later, other tankers that were part of the lightering operation—had to sit very close to the rocky reef. These ships were in a dangerous place.

Saturday dawned as another beautiful, calm day, but no one in Prince William Sound was enjoying the weather. Out at the wreck, divers entered the oil-covered water to examine the damage and assess what kind of danger the ship was in. One foot (0.3 m) of oil on the surface of the water blotted out the sunlight, leaving the water below in total darkness. One of the divers described what he saw in the light of his headlamp:

> We felt our way in the darkness while this enormous ship was creaking and groaning. The hull is seven-eighths-inch [2.2-cm] steel, but it was like a tin can with holes punched in it. Big chunks of metal were hanging down. There were dozens of holes, some large enough to drive a truck through.

If the ship slipped off the rocks, it would roll over within 30 to 90 seconds and sink.

Frank Iarossi, who had flown in from Houston, now knew that the ship was in real danger of capsizing and spilling the 1 million barrels of oil that remained in its cargo tanks. He was determined not to let that happen. As president of Exxon Shipping, Iarossi made the difficult decision to proceed with the lightering operation, knowing the dangers. As he explained later, "We had a 240,000-barrel problem. And the last thing in the world we could stand is having a 1,240,000-barrel problem." Two Coast Guard boats stood by in case the tanker broke up and the crew had to be rescued. Almost four-fifths of the total oil carried by the *Exxon Valdez* was transferred to tankers and removed.

The Disaster Gets Worse

The cleanup of the spreading oil slick was not going well. When the Alyeska response team had finally arrived on Friday afternoon, it had only enough equipment to clean up a spill of 10,000 gallons (37,800 l)—hardly enough to handle the 11 million gallons (41.6 million l) that had already spilled. Exxon then announced that it was taking over responsibility for the cleanup from Alyeska. Exxon would be in charge. Iarossi knew that his company did not have enough equipment to clean a spill this large mechanically. He wanted to use faster methods, but they were controversial and required state approval. One method was to use fire, and the other was to use chemicals.

When an oil slick is set on fire, the fire consumes the oil, using it as its own fuel. But setting fire to an oil slick creates a lot of hazards. Toxic fumes are released into the environment, and tankers, other boats, and everything else near the oil slick has to be protected from the fire. The only safe place to start an oil fire is far from shore and also far from the oil surrounding the tankers. By late Saturday, approvals and equipment were ready for a burn test. Two ships dragging a line of special fireproof booms corralled a section of oil and towed it off to be burned. This burn was a suc-

cess. In the end, however, only 15,000 gallons (56,760 l) of oil were removed from the water this way, because the rest of the oil weathered further, and once oil has weathered, it no longer burns.

This plane is releasing dispersants over the Exxon Valdez *oil spill in Prince William Sound. Dispersants proved to be unsuccessful in cleaning up the oil due to stormy weather conditions. (Photo courtesy of Associated Press)*

Exxon officials pinned their hopes on chemicals called *dispersants*. A dispersant is a kind of detergent that breaks up an oil slick into droplets. Then the droplets no longer float on the surface—they sink down or disperse into the seawater. These chemicals could make as much as 30 percent of the oil slick disappear.

Many scientists, officials, and environmentalists considered this chemical solution too toxic. Environmentalists say that dispersants do not really clean up the oil. The oil is still in the environment—it is just not as visible. Worse yet, in the first six hours after the chemicals are applied, the toll on marine life living below an oil slick is huge.

Near shorelines where marine life was concentrated, the possible use of dispersants caused heated and lengthy arguments. As first Alyeska and then Exxon argued with the state for permission to use the chemicals, critical hours ticked by. To work well, dispersants must be applied within the first 18 to 24 hours after a spill. Beyond that period, weathering begins to make the oil too thick and gooey for the chemicals to break up. Finally, Alyeska was given permission by the Alaska Department of Environmental Conservation (DEC) and the U.S. *Environmental Protection Agency* (EPA) to test dispersants on a small area of the spill. This way, if they did not work well, the potential danger of introducing large amounts of chemicals into the environment could be avoided.

The first test was authorized on Friday afternoon, and by 6:00 P.M. (AKST), the first dispersants were dropped from a helicopter. The beautiful, calm weather did not help this operation. Like detergent in a washing machine, dispersants work best in turbulence. The test was not successful. A dispersant-spraying plane was flown in from Arizona, and more tests were made on Saturday, but they continued to show poor results.

In a coordinated cleanup effort, dispersants are placed on oil previously contained by booms. (Photo courtesy of Associated Press)

By Sunday morning (which happened to be Easter), the oil slick stretched over 100 square miles (259 km²). Later that day, the governor of Alaska, Steve Cowper, declared a state of emergency, and the National Guard was brought out to help. According to Alyeska's plan, 100,000 barrels of oil should have been recovered by this time, but in fact, fewer than 3,000 barrels had been collected.

By the end of the afternoon, burning operations were planned, and the use of dispersants was agreed upon for one region of the oil slick. The calm weather was starting to change, and the seas were choppy, helping the dispersants used in the tests to work. Exxon flew in crews that specialized in the use of dispersants. Skimmers, booms, and tons of chemicals were rushed to the scene. The bulk of the cleanup, it appeared, was finally ready to get started.

But overnight, the weather became nightmarish. Howling winds gusting up to 73 miles (117 km) per hour blew the preceding day's plans apart. The burning operation had been canceled late the previous evening. Planes that were to spray dispersants were grounded. Boats and skimmers had to head for shelter.

Out on Bligh Reef, even the lightering operation was threatened. Four strong tugboats tried to keep the rafted tankers in position, but the winds spun the *Exxon Valdez* and the *Exxon Baton Rouge,* which was now full of oil, 12 degrees over the rocky reef.

Pushed by the wind, the oil sped over 20 miles (32 km) in one day. Frank Iarossi described its movement this way: "The slick is moving like it's on a superhighway. Our worst fears happened. The wind just shot us down. Those winds stampeded the slick out of the center of the sound over to the islands."

Rough seas turned the oil to mousse and then tossed the toxic goo 40 feet (12 m) up onto pristine shores and beaches. Mousse does not burn. Dispersants would no longer work, and the area of the disaster grew too big for the world's largest oil company to clean up. By the end of the day, the slick covered 500 square miles (1,295 km²).

CHAPTER 3

Death and Rescue

In newspapers and magazines and on television, people around the world saw pictures of rocky Alaskan shores coated in thick, sticky oil. Shown in these pictures were baby harbor seals covered in brown, sticky mousse; dead and dying *murres* (a type of seabird) with their white breast feathers blackened by oil; and grown men and women crying as they pulled dying sea otters from the water. The images of dead and dying animals pushed thousands of people into action. Schoolchildren raised money, scientists offered their expertise, and men and women from every walk of life volunteered to come and do whatever was needed to rescue the animals.

This photo shows some of the many shorebirds exposed to oil that would perish from oil poisoning and hypothermia. (Photo courtesy of National Oceanic and Atmospheric Administration)

Few places in North America have more wildlife to lose than Prince William Sound in the spring. Over 30 species of mammals live on the surrounding land, including black bears, deer, foxes, wolves, mountain goats, and minks. These animals live quite undisturbed by the modern world in the sweet-smelling forests of evergreen spruce trees.

Along with spring come the birds—millions of them. Great flocks of migrating seabirds, waterfowl, and shorebirds arrive in March, April, May, and June. Many swans, ducks, and geese are winging their way north at this time. Seabirds such as murres and *loons* arrive by the hundreds of thousands. Other birds live near the sound year-round. More than 2,000 majestic bald eagles live along the shores, returning to the same nests year after year. These great hunters snatch fish from the seawater and rodents from the forests.

Each spring, the watery world of the sound becomes a giant playpen where marine mammals come to raise their young. Walruses and huge sea lions weighing up to 1 ton (0.9 mt) raise their pups on the rocky islands that dot the region. Smaller seals weighing about 250 pounds (113 kg) also return. The beautiful harbor seals live in the sound year-round, although even before the spill, the number of harbor seals was in decline.

One of the most common marine mammals in the area was the beautiful sea otter. After years of being hunted for its thick fur, it was endangered. In 1989 the greatest concentration of sea otters in North America—over 12,000, and maybe as many as 20,000—lived on Prince William Sound. These mammals romp in the waters year-round, sticking close to the kelp beds where they hide if they spy a killer whale in the area. (The "Sea Otters" sidebar on the following page tells more about the habits of otters.) Killer whales, along with huge humpback whales and porpoises, return each spring with their calves to fatten up on the bounty of fish, shrimp, and other creatures living in the water—and the bounty of marine life is great. (The killer whales are highlighted in "The Prince William Whale Pod" sidebar on page 28.)

Sea Otters

Before the turn of the 20th century, sea otters could be seen playing all along northern Pacific shores, but their thick fur caused them to be hunted almost to extinction by 1911. These fun-loving, social animals live in groups known as rafts or pods that number from just a few to several hundred animals. Sea otters are the largest members of the weasel family. The common weasel prefers to spend its days and nights on solid ground, but sea otters love the water. They hunt, eat, play, and even sleep in water. To eat at sea, an otter lies on its back and places its dinner on its chest, which it uses as a table. If dinner is a clam, the otter places a rock on its chest, and, holding the clam with both paws, cracks the morsel open on the rock.

From March to June, 15 million salmon swim into Prince William Sound on a journey to the streams and rivers where they were born. They return to spawn, or lay their eggs. Five species of Pacific salmon return to the sound after spending two to six years at sea. Huge schools of herring, halibut, haddock, sable fish, and many more are abundant in the sound waters. Big crabs, as well as shrimps, mussels, clams, and squid, also make the sound their home.

The spill could hardly have happened in a worse place or at a worse time of year for the animals. People began finding dead and dying animals on the first day of the disaster. As the oil spread, so did the death toll. One rescue worker described the scene: "It's just beyond imagination. Oil everywhere. Snow falling. Dead otters. Dead deer. Dead birds." The communities of people who lived on the shore of the sound watched the shoreline become a death zone.

Saving the Otters

The sea otters instantly became a symbol of the spill. Seeing such cute creatures covered in oil and struggling for life horrified and angered people across the nation and around the world. In one day, the governor's office received 2,000 calls from people who wanted to help.

One such person was Suzanne Marinelli, who came from Hawaii with friends. She said, "I thought maybe I could make just a little difference. I decided I had to go. Sometimes you've just got to take a leap of faith." Marinelli worked cleaning otters at one of the rescue centers that were set up and funded by the Exxon Corporation. "Volunteers had come from all over the country," she explained. "Minnesota, Colorado, New York, Texas, Florida…lots of them from the West Coast states. We worked alongside people from Australia, Germany, Switzerland, and China too."

Otters are very vulnerable to oil. One-quarter of the population was considered dead or dying in the first weeks of the spill. Usually, an otter's thick fur traps warm air next to the skin, insulating the animal from the icy waters of the sound. But when an

Sea otters, one of the most beloved animals found in Prince William Sound, were hit hard by the spill, because the oil prevented their bodies' natural heating systems from functioning properly. (Photo courtesy of Associated Press)

The Prince William Whale Pod

People familiar with life in Prince William Sound know the pod, or group, of killer whales that returns each year. There were once 22 members in the pod, each with its own family history and personality. Some even had nicknames, such as a big male named Eyak. Killer whales have no natural enemies, so they often live to be 50 to 80 years old. However, these whales began dying after the *Exxon Valdez* spill. Since then, the number of deaths in this pod is more than has ever been seen in a killer whale pod.

In the years after the spill, nine whales were lost—and today, they continue to die. By 2004, the pod had lost 14 of its members. Concerned citizens have organized to try to find a way to help the pod survive. They hope to get special protection for the Prince William pod under the Marine Mammal Protection Act of 1972, which was established to protect marine mammals living in U.S. waters.

otter pops its head up through oil-covered water, its fur soaks up the oil like a sponge. Oiled fur no longer traps air, so it no longer keeps the otter warm. The animal begins to grow cold and soon dies of this condition, called *hypothermia*. Other otters are poisoned when they try to lick the oil from their fur. Ingesting oil causes liver or kidney failure.

Rescue teams went out in boats chartered by Exxon to collect otters from the oil-covered water and beaches. Local citizens brought in many more otters in pet carriers or cardboard boxes. As soon as an otter was brought to a rescue center, it was bathed in warm water. The bath warmed the animal up and removed the oil. At the same time, the otter's mouth was held open and a mixture of dissolved charcoal and nutrients was squirted down its throat. The charcoal absorbed any oil in the otter's stomach, preventing the animal from being poisoned. Then the otter was rinsed and finally dried with towels and hair dryers.

Dealing with otters can be difficult. They weigh 30 pounds (13.6 kg), they are wild, and they come in very scared. Many rescue workers received nasty bites as they worked. Once cleaned, the otters were put in airline animal carriers and carefully watched.

Marinelli described what she did next. "My job was taking care of twelve otters in six pens. I fed them and cleaned their pens, I watched them grooming, splashing in the water.... I wanted to make each of these little hurt beings feel better."

About half the otters in the rescue centers died, in spite of everyone's best efforts. The dead otters were taken out the back door, away from the media. Exxon officials were especially concerned about cute otters dying in front of news cameras. People were angry and blamed Exxon for the terrible death toll. Exxon officials did what they could—they paid for everything that might help the otters recover. They even flew in fresh oysters, clams, mussels, and crabs for the otters to eat. The price was high—$60 per otter per day.

Bird Rescue

Rescuers also brought birds to the rescue centers. Among the worst hit were the seabirds. One horrified witness described an encounter with a loon:

> We heard a noise. It was a loon—a big loon. All we could see was its head sticking up out of the oil. Its eyes were red and it made that eerie loon call. I grabbed him and pulled him out of the sludge. He was just covered....
> I mean, I couldn't even hold onto him. The loon was sliding out of my hands and biting me.

Much like an otter's fur, a bird's fluffy feathers trap warm air next to the skin. Oil-soaked feathers become heavy and no longer

Pelicans were among the many birds affected by the oil spill because they preyed on other animals already poisoned by oil. (Photo courtesy of National Oceanic and Atmospheric Administration)

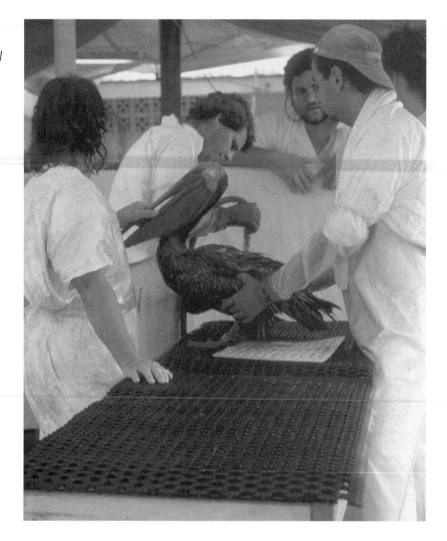

work. The bird cannot fly and its body grows cold. When the bird tries to clean the oil from its feathers, it is poisoned.

To clean the oil off a rescued bird, volunteers first dunked it in warm soapy water and scrubbed every feather with a toothbrush. To clean around the bird's eyes, volunteers used a water pick—the same kind that people use to clean around their teeth. Then the bird was rinsed. Often, this process had to be repeated more than once. Being handled causes stress to a wild animal such as a loon. Many birds died even after they were cleaned.

Death of an Ecosystem

An ecosystem is a community of plants, animals, and other organisms that interact with each other and their nonliving environment—such as water and rock. When all these elements are balanced, ecosystems are self-sufficient. The plants and animals that live in an ecosystem, and decomposers such as fungi and bacteria—that feed on and break down dead plant or animal matter—provide all the nutrients that an ecosystem needs. All an ecosystem must get from the outside is energy, which is usually provided by the Sun. Ecosystems generally change very slowly over time, but a disaster can change an ecosystem suddenly and drastically. This is what happened in Prince William Sound.

The first animals to die—the otters and seabirds—were the ones that dove through the floating mass of oil. The cycle of death did not end there. People began finding dead eagles lying beneath their nests, seemingly untouched by oil. Dead deer, bears, foxes, and mink were found. The death zone was spreading. What was happening?

Biologists were among the first people on the scene. Everyone knew that gathering information from this spill would be important to the future, so they came to observe and measure how this much oil, spilled into a pristine environment, would change the whole ecosystem. What they learned was troubling.

When oil spills into the water, it coats the kelp, pop weed, and eelgrass—plants that grow in the water near the shore. When deer browse on the eelgrass, they are poisoned and may die. Bears eat carrion, or dead animals. When a bear eats a dead deer, the bear is poisoned and may die. If the bear has nursing cubs, her cubs will also die. These animals all die because there is oil on the eelgrass, even though the animals may not have touched the plants themselves. They are all part of a food chain that has been poisoned.

Every animal in an ecosystem is part of a food chain, but the *Exxon Valdez* poisoned many of the food chains around Prince

William Sound. The dead eagles had eaten contaminated fish or rodents that had consumed contaminated plants. The dead wolves and foxes probably had eaten carrion such as dead deer. The dead mink might have killed and eaten dying seabirds. In an ecosystem, the health of each organism affects the health of other organisms.

Death is not the only result of an oil spill. Another result is lowered reproduction rates. For example, sea algae are plantlike organisms that grow in Prince William Sound. If the sea algae do not reproduce well or bloom, sea urchins have less food. With fewer sea urchins available, otters, crabs, fish, ducks, and seagulls go hungry. If the number of otters declines, there is less food for killer whales. The *Exxon Valdez* oil spill set off such a chain reaction, and no one really knew how it would end. In Prince William

It is hypothesized that the whale population that migrates through the waters of Prince William Sound was affected by the Exxon Valdez *oil spill as 13 members of one killer whale pod died in the year and a half following the disaster. (Photo courtesy of Associated Press)*

Sound, the whole ecosystem seemed to be collapsing. At a restaurant called the Reluctant Fisherman Inn, a sign was posted that read, "Flags are at half-mast due to the death of our environment."

When the scientists counted the number of dead animals, the totals were staggering. The number of dead otters counted was 1,016. An unbelievable 36,460 seabirds—mostly murres—were counted. On land, 151 dead eagles were found, but eagles usually go deep into remote regions of the forest to die, so no one knows the actual number of eagles that were killed. Of the eagles that survived, few were able to reproduce that year. Since most of the animals that died had drowned and were never found, scientists estimate the death toll at 350,000 to 390,000 seabirds, 2,650 sea otters, and 300 harbor seals. Many experts estimate that more than half of the wild animals in Prince William Sound died in the disaster.

CHAPTER 4

The Cleanup

Exxon was criticized for using high-temperature, high-pressure water to clean the beaches. Many experts thought that the technique could do as much damage to the environment in Prince William Sound as the oil spill. (Photo courtesy of Associated Press)

On day four, when storm waves first threw the thick, sticky mousse up onto the beaches, the DEC notified Exxon that beach cleanup crews would be needed. The operation to clean beaches would be added to the lightering operation, several animal rescue operations, and the mechanical, chemical, and burning operations on the oil slick. The Exxon Corporation was fighting many battles at once. The company needed more people, and it was willing to pay good wages for them.

People came from far and near. In Pennsylvania, Don Jones climbed into his pickup truck and began the drive of more than 5,000 miles (8,045 km) to Valdez. He would work handing out socks, gloves, and foul weather gear to the cleanup crews. In Hawaii, a Frenchwoman named Cecile boarded a jet to Alaska, where she would work as a cook feeding the cleanup crews. Many of the local fishers were hired for various jobs, such as ferrying people in their boats or cleaning beaches. They did not know if there would be a fishing season that year, they needed the money, and they wanted to do something—anything—to save the marine environment which they depended upon for the fish that they caught.

Exxon hired and trained 11,000 men and women, and the pay was good—workers received $16.69 an hour for cleaning the beaches. Large barges were turned into housing for those workers who needed it. These floating hotels were nicknamed "floatels." Some workers, like Don Jones, saved their housing allowance of $35 per day and brought their own "housing"—Jones lived in his truck. Exxon also chartered 1,400 boats and 85 aircraft to transport the cleanup crews, scientists, news reporters, volunteers, and officials to the many shores and islands that could be reached no other way. These expenses mounted to a whopping $10 million a day—all paid for by Exxon.

Unfortunately, as the days and weeks came and went, the crisis just kept spreading. Money could not solve this problem. By day seven, the oil slick had moved out of the sound and into the Pacific Ocean, where currents carried it along Alaska's scenic southern coast. By week five, the spill covered 6,000 square miles (15,500 km^2)—an area a little smaller than that of the state of Massachusetts. By June, the oil slicks had spread out over 10,000 square miles (25,900 km^2).

In addition to the swarms of Exxon employees, volunteers, and relief workers, hundreds of journalists and radio and television crews descended upon Valdez and the surrounding towns. In some ways this was good. The press reported to the world what was taking place in Valdez, ensuring that Exxon would behave with accountability. But media coverage also added to the frustration that many company officials felt. Exxon leaders believed that precious cleanup time was often wasted because they had to answer questions posed by the media at lengthy, twice-daily press conferences.

Help from Afar

Foreign countries offered their help. Norway, halfway around the world, had some large skimmers and offered to bring them, but the boats were too far away to get to Alaska in time to be of help. Alaska's neighbor to the west, the Soviet Union (present-day

On April 9, 1989, off Knight Island in Prince William Sound, one of many small fishing boats used in the cleanup effort contains part of the oil slick as a skimming barge (top) sucks up the oil. (Photo courtesy of Associated Press)

Russia), offered to send the biggest skimmer ship in the world. The skimmer ship was called the *Vaydaghubsky,* and it was only five days away in Siberia. U.S. government agencies were not happy about a ship from a Communist country entering the United States, but eventually, the ship steamed into Alaskan waters flying the flags of the United States and the Soviet Union. The *Vaydaghubsky* was designed to scoop up 200,000 gallons (756,800 l) of oil per hour.

The big Soviet ship went to work along with 12 other skimmers—many of which had been flown in from around the United States—and the mechanical recovery of oil continued. However, the sticky mousse clogged all of the skimmers, even the *Vaydaghubsky.* If all these skimmers had been on-site during the first three days of calm weather, before the oil was churned into mousse, they could have made a real difference.

Only the *supersuckers* succeeded on the mousse. A supersucker is a large vacuum truck built to clean up oil spills on land. Jack Lamb, a fisher from the village of Cordova, got a driver to bring one of these trucks from the oil fields in the north down to Prince William Sound. The truck was then mounted on a barge and taken to one of the worst sites in the sound. The supersucker worked. Subsequently, in the month after the storm, supersuckers removed 450,000 gallons (1.7 million l) of mousse from the sea. But mousse is 80 percent water, so only 20 percent of the mousse—about 90,000 gallons (340,600 l)—was oil. Although that seems like a lot of oil, it amounted to only 0.82 percent of the oil spilled. The "Spilled Oil" sidebar above tells more about the collection and disposal of oil.

Spilled Oil

Spilled oil is not only troublesome to collect, but also difficult to dispose of. Some of the spilled oil and mousse that were collected by skimmers and supersuckers in Prince William Sound were dumped into a storage barge. This barge delivered the oil and mousse to a water separator. Once the water and oil were separated from each other, much of the oil was loaded into barrels and shipped to the port of Tacoma, Washington. From there, it was trucked to a toxic waste dump in Arlington, Oregon.

Cleaning the Beaches

Most oil spills are easier to clean than the one in Prince William Sound. The cold temperatures in Alaska preserved the oil. In warmer climates, oil weathers and breaks down much more quickly. Also, oils are not all the same. Oil from Alaska is more toxic than other oils. This oil takes longer to break down than most other oils, so it stays in the environment longer.

As difficult as it was removing oil from the sea, cleaning oil from miles of rocky shoreline was a much more difficult job. The stone and gravel beaches absorb oil, which then slowly leaks back into the water and onto new beaches. Further, Prince William Sound is an inlet of the Gulf of Alaska, which is about 2,500 square miles (6,475 km²) of water, reefs, and islands. The sound has an incredible 3,000 miles (4,830 km) of shoreline twisting along the mainland and circling the many islands.

At first, Exxon began the beach-cleaning operations using specially heavy and absorbent paper towels. Teams of people on a beach picked up each stone, wiped it off, and then put it back. The work was slow, and beaches cleaned this way were often oiled again as the tides came and went. Meanwhile, reports of more oily shorelines poured in. Eventually, more than 1,000 miles (1,610 km) of rocky shoreline were covered with the pudding-like brown mousse. Wiping oil from rocks by hand was like washing a truck with a toothbrush during a dust storm.

Exxon workers began washing mousse from the rocks using high-pressure, cold-water hoses. This method cleaned the shore, but it made the oil stickier, thicker, and much harder to collect. Finally high-pressure hoses were used with hot water. These made the shores look cleaner. The oil was hosed to the water's edge, where it pooled, trapped by booms floating just beyond the shore. Then skimmers scooped up the oil and removed it from the environment. Exxon's cleanup crews would spend a day blasting the oil from a beach and then move on. At the height of the cleanup, Exxon had

3,500 people using 200 million gallons (757 million l) of high-pressured water per day on the beaches of Prince William Sound.

While the use of hot water on the shores certainly worked to remove some oil, scientists became worried that using hot water caused a whole new set of problems. The area between the high tide and low tide marks along a shore is called the *intertidal zone*. Biologists said that 90 percent of the snails, mussels, and other organisms living in this zone were being killed by the cleanup. Other scientists noted that the use of high-pressure hoses forced oil deeper into the gravel and under the rocks. Oil that is exposed to sunlight and air continues to break down, but oil that is buried is protected from the elements that weather it, so it remains in the environment longer.

The sandy coastline of Prince William Sound was especially difficult to clean because the tide continually brought in new deposits of oil. As soon as workers completed cleaning the sand, a new slick of oil would cover the beach again. (Photo courtesy of National Oceanic and Atmospheric Administration)

To prevent these problems, Exxon restricted the use of hot water to only the most heavily oiled shorelines. On other shores, cleanup crews returned to hand-washing. They also began using big, heavy equipment such as backhoes and front-end loaders to dig up the oil-soaked gravel in order to wash it out.

After weeks and weeks of cleaning, not one shoreline was actually clean. Exxon began to say that a beach had been "treated" instead of using the term "cleaned." Although the operation was big and expensive, it was not very successful. Then scientists at Alaska's Institute of Marine Science made a discovery. Bacteria that lived in the seawater were consuming some of the oil in the water. There were not enough of these organisms to make much difference, but scientists suggested adding additional microbes. Using living organisms to clean the environment is called *bioremediation*. As William Reilly of the EPA said, "It's natural. It's promising. It's based on good, sound science. They are native Alaskan bugs."

The government and Exxon together funded research to find out if bioremediation would really work. The researchers found that in order to be effective, the oil-eating organisms needed a lot of nitrogen and phosphorous. Both of these natural elements are found in fertilizer, so for a test, fertilizer was spread on an oiled beach. After a month, some EPA researchers said that the oil-eating bacteria were effective and that the test was a success. Other scientists were not convinced.

No one really knew what loading the environment with phosphorus and nitrogen would do to the whole ecosystem. Then the phosphorus in the fertilizer started to make the people spreading it on the beaches sick. This was not a good sign. Phosphorus is toxic to humans, and the fumes began to cause internal bleeding and liver and kidney damage. In the end, bioremediation was only used on beaches that met certain requirements—there had to be enough movement of the water to make the water mix with and dilute the added nitrogen and phosphorus.

Criticism of Exxon's Cleanup Methods

As the summer wore on, many local people became increasingly frustrated and angry with Exxon. The priorities of the giant corporation were often at odds with the priorities of the fishers, local citizens, and state and federal officials. Officials started to complain that Exxon seemed more worried about the lawsuits that were pending than anything else. Fishers who labored on the cleanup crews thought that Exxon was more concerned with its image in the media than with cleaning the environment.

In one incident, a large crew of workers was flown by helicopter to a remote oil-covered beach just hours before a *USA Today* television crew arrived. The workers cleaned the oil from the rocks for as long as the television cameras filmed the work. Immediately after the TV crew left, the entire cleanup operation stopped and the workers were flown back out. When asked about the incident, one worker said, "Exxon was definitely putting on a show."

Criticism of Exxon and its methods grew. Some people believed that the use of chemicals, high-pressure hoses, and enormous groups of workers unfamiliar with the fragile terrain could cause further injury to the shoreline. After hearing rumors that

The increase in the population of Valdez and surrounding towns put additional pressure on the area's services. In this photo, loads of garbage wait to be shipped out. (Photo courtesy of National Oceanic and Atmospheric Administration)

the high-tech cleanup operations were doing more damage than good, Congressman Wayne Owens from Utah traveled to Alaska unannounced to have a look around for himself. He dressed in the rugged clothing worn by fishers, and no one took much notice of him. He talked to the people working on the cleanup crews, he talked to local residents, and he went to the cleanup sites to observe what was really happening. Back in Washington, D.C., in a congressional committee meeting, Owens publicly addressed Bill Stevens, president of Exxon U.S.A.:

> I am one who believes that much of your high-tech oper-ation is doing more damage than good. In Northwest Bay...where I visited ten days ago, you have 400 to 500 people in thirty-five to forty-five vessels. Unannounced, I talked to your foreman there, after having reviewed a lot of what's going on with all of those high-pressure, 160-degree [Fahrenheit] [71°C] water hoses, and after seeing all those boats plying that beautiful pristine—pre-viously pristine—harbor. And I said to him, "How much oil are you collecting here with this massive operation?"
>
> His answer was seven barrels of oil a day. I can't imagine that the [impact] of 400 to 500 people...can be offset by the seven barrels of oil that's being recov-ered. It's the high-tech part of what you're doing up there that bothers me.

Less invasive, low-tech solutions to collecting oil had been tried and proven by local fishers and other Alaskans. During Owens's visit, he was shown how the mousse could be scooped up from the water and dumped into a bucket using a simple rake fitted with a piece of screen. Owens said,

> Your foreman showed me how hand implements really work much better than those big supersuckers.... I'd like to see somebody go into Snug Harbor, where I

picked up an eagle feather in a pool of oil that had not yet been treated. I'd like to see a couple of people go in, in a shallow draft boat, with three buckets and one of these jerry-built [homemade] devices…and very quietly clean up those horrible pools of oil. I'm afraid you're going to send a multimillion-dollar operation in. And I'm afraid it's going to do more damage than good.

However, Exxon refused to use these methods. The oil company did not see how average people using rags, rakes, and buckets could treat a spill of this size. According to some locals, Exxon believed that the images of the slow-going, labor-intensive work were bad for business. The company wanted to appear to have better resources to remedy this disaster in an efficient, speedy way.

As the summer of 1989 came to an end, Exxon announced that its cleanup operation would close on September 15. People were surprised. There was still plenty of oil in the environment. But Exxon held firm, declaring that it had "treated" 700 miles (1,130 km) of beaches and removed as much oil as possible from Prince William Sound. Over 50,000 tons (45,400 mt) of oil-soaked material had been shipped to the toxic waste dump in Oregon. The job was done, Exxon said. The company would review the state of the beaches next spring before it made a decision to return. Many environmentalists, biologists, and local Alaskans were not sorry to see Exxon go.

Local residents, with help from the state government, renewed a cleanup operation the next spring. Exxon agreed to send in a much smaller workforce of about 1,000 people to aid the local effort. In April 1990, 150 people in a low-tech operation quietly picked up oily waste from the shorelines—128,000 pounds (58,100 kg) of it.

In June 1992, the cleanup was finally declared complete—three years and three months after the *Exxon Valdez* had run aground on Bligh Reef. Yet even after the cleanup, people taking a walk in a tidal marsh could find oil simply by looking into their own footprints.

A Mearns Rock Photo Essay

Mearns Rock is a boulder about 4 feet (1.2 m) high and 7 feet (2.1 m) long located on a south-facing rocky shoreline of Knight Island in Prince William Sound. The boulder falls in the intertidal zone of Snug Harbor. Waves wash up over the rock as the tide comes in and back over it as the tide recedes.

Fifteen months after the spill, the surface of Mearns Rock is covered by algae. Barnacles and mussels are also scattered over parts of the rock. (Photos courtesy of National Oceanic and Atmospheric Administration)

Five years after the spill, the mussel colony is smaller, but it is unclear if the decrease in size is due to oil pollution or natural causes. (Photos courtesy of National Oceanic and Atmospheric Administration)

Mearns Rock and the Knight Island shoreline were covered with oil from the *Exxon Valdez* spill. This particular area was never treated or cleaned after the spill. For the past 14 years, biologists have photographed this boulder once a year, usually in the early summer. They do this to study the effects that natural processes (such as weather and waves) have upon the recovery of

New species of seaweed are growing on Mearns Rock in 2000, and eelgrass is beginning to thrive in the surrounding water. (Photos courtesy of National Oceanic and Atmospheric Administration)

Mearns Rock is clear of new colonies of mussels or algae. Growth in sea lettuce can be seen along the corner of the boulder. (Photo courtesy of National Oceanic and Atmospheric Administration)

a site after an oil spill. On the previous pages is a selection of photographs taken through the years, showing varieties of marine life on and around the boulder.

At high tide, only the top portion of the rock is visible. This photo, taken 15 months after the oil spill, shows the surface of the rock covered with algae. Barnacles are visible on the whitish section on the right of the rock. The dark patch on the right indicates a growing mussel colony. No oil is visible on the surface of the rock.

Five years later, Mearns Rock is photographed at low tide. The mussel colony is much smaller, maybe due to otters foraging for food or other natural causes. At this time, it cannot yet be concluded that oil has had an effect on reproductive rates of the mussel species. There is fresh algae growth on the beach side of the rock, indicating the resurgence of new life.

New species of seaweed can now be seen on the rock at low tide. The seaweed and algae hide colonies of barnacles and mussels. Upon close inspection, eelgrass can be seen in the water surrounding the boulder. The algae plants have reached maturity, but there is no sign of new growth.

In 2003 there are fewer barnacles and no new colonies of mussels or algae. Sea lettuce grows along the left corner of the rock.

According to the photographs taken of Mearns Rock, all surface oil disappeared within four years of the *Exxon Valdez* spill. Because this section of shoreline is well protected from wind and harsh waves, it is likely that there is residual oil below the surface. This may be the reason that mussel and algae colonies have not reproduced as vigorously as before the spill. Clearly, however, toxic levels in the water are low enough to allow other intertidal species to flourish. Biologists, geologists, and chemists will continue to study Mearns Rock and other areas of shoreline along Prince William Sound for years to come in order to understand the continuing effects of oil spills on the marine environment.

CHAPTER 5

A Community in Crisis

Cordova, Alaska, is a remote village on Prince William Sound that can be reached only by small plane or by boat. No roads link the community to the rest of the world, so anyone who tries to drive out of town soon has to turn around and go back. This isolation makes Cordova a tight-knit place.

Most of the year, about 2,600 people live in Cordova, but during the fishing season, the population usually swells to about 4,500 people. Small as it is, Cordova was ranked the ninth-leading

The oil spill had severe, permanent effects on the economy and psychology of the townspeople in Cordova, Alaska, on Prince William Sound. (Photo courtesy of Steve Kaufman/ CORBIS)

port in the nation for commercial fish harvest before the spill. Directly or indirectly, just about everyone in town depends on fish. Those who do not actually fish work in fishing-related businesses such as packing and canning fish, mending the long fishing nets, or repairing and maintaining the many fishing boats.

Just about everyone in Cordova knew that an oil spill would be a disaster. Grassroots organizations and other members of the community actively tried to prevent the Trans-Alaska Pipeline from coming to Prince William Sound by lobbying the state and federal government. There were other, safer ways, they said, to get North Slope oil to the "lower forty-eight," as Alaskans call the 48 states to the south of them.

Why not build a pipeline across Canada and into the United States? Then there would be no danger of polluting the bays and seas that so many Alaskans depended on for their livelihoods. Environmentalists and Cordova fishers pointed out that in 1964, the Great Alaska Earthquake—measuring 8.4 on the Richter scale—shook the region around Prince William Sound and beyond, to Anchorage, causing one of the worst environmental disasters of the day. Oil storage tanks in towns such as Seward and Kodiak burst into flames and spilled burning oil that polluted birds' nesting grounds and killed fish, shellfish, and algae. According to the National Academy of Science, "Few earthquakes in history have altered life environments so profoundly and over so large an area," and geologists agreed that another earthquake was likely. See "The Great Alaska Earthquake" sidebar on the following page for more on this quake.

However, American oil companies wanted to keep the pipeline within the United States. A terminal port in Prince William Sound was the best solution, the companies said. The sound was a perfect harbor for supertankers because it was protected from the big waves of the Pacific Ocean, it was the only harbor in the United States deep enough for supertankers, and its waters rarely froze over during the winter.

The Great Alaska Earthquake

On March 27, 1964, the most powerful earthquake ever recorded on the North American continent struck in Alaska. Its epicenter was just about midway between Valdez and the city of Anchorage. In Anchorage, buildings split in half, and streets and pavements dropped as much as 30 feet (9.1 m). In Valdez, the ground heaved, toppling power lines. As the lines fell, they sparked, igniting tanks of fuel oil. Out in the sound, the sea bottom shifted violently, pushing millions of tons of water into a great wave—a *tsunami*—at least 30 feet (9.1 m) high. The wave rushed toward Valdez, lifting the 10,000-ton (9,070-mt) ship SS *Chena* into the air as it smashed ashore. Just as quickly, the waters washed out, pulling the pier, cars, trucks, and those people that could not escape with it. Similar scenes occurred around the sound as the huge waves sloshed back and forth. Beyond the sound, the waves rushed across open water, causing hundreds of deaths and $400 million in damage along the shores of North America, on the Hawaiian Islands, and beyond.

To win over Alaskans, Alyeska made lots of promises. The consortium promised clean air, clean water, and state-of-the-art pollution technology. One of its top pollution specialists promised that Alyeska's plan would

> detail methods for dealing promptly and effectively with any oil spill which may occur, so that its effects on the environment will be minimal. We have adequate knowledge for dealing with oil spills. . . . The best equipment, materials, and expertise . . . will make operation in the Port of Valdez and Prince William Sound the safest in the world.

North Slope oil brought billions of dollars to the state and the people of Alaska. Eventually, most of the people of Cordova were resigned to the pipeline's existence. But on the fateful Thursday night, as North Slope crude was being pumped into the cargo tanks of the *Exxon Valdez*, a woman named Riki Ott was speaking to a Valdez town meeting about the likelihood of a really big oil spill in Prince William Sound. Ott was on the board of directors of the Cordova District Fishermen United (CDFU), the fishers' union. She is an expert on oil pollution and poisonous sediment. That evening, she spoke to the fishers and concerned citizens in Valdez. "Given the high frequency of tankers into Port Valdez, the increasing age and size of that tanker fleet, and the inability to quickly contain and clean up an oil spill in the open water of Alaska, fishermen feel that we are playing a game of Russian roulette," she said. "It's not a matter of *if*. It's just a matter of *when* we get the big one."

Riki Ott in Action

Stuck in Cordova because the weather was too foggy to fly out that night, Ott addressed the meeting that was taking place in Valdez by speaking into a telecommunications microphone. The mayor of Valdez, John Devens, had called the meeting because of his concerns over oil spills. After a small oil spill in January, at the terminal in the Port of Valdez, Alyeska had appeared understaffed and unprepared. Budget cuts had reduced the size and expertise of the staff and the technical and mechanical resources available in an emergency. Cleanup of the 72,000 gallons (272,400 l) that had leaked from the tanker *Thompson Pass* had taken two weeks. The mayor had asked Ott to speak because, in addition to holding a salmon fishing permit, she also had a master's degree in oil pollution. After the meeting, Ott rode her bicycle home and went to sleep.

The next morning, Jack Lamb banged on Ott's door and yelled for her to wake up. Lamb was another leader of the CDFU. The Union Hall was the head and heart of the Cordova community. Whenever anything big happened, people gathered there. At 7:00 A.M. (AKST), when Lamb learned of the spill, he went straight to the hall and called Ott. Her phone was off the hook, so he went to her house to get her.

In 1993, activist Riki Ott was still in action protecting the people of Prince William Sound. In this photograph, Marie Smith Jones (right), a member of the Eyak tribe, thanks Ott for her efforts protesting logging in the area. (Photo courtesy of Natalie Forbes/ CORBIS)

Lamb and Ott went back to the Union Hall, and along with the union's director, Marilyn Leland, they immediately started their own rescue operation. Ott hitched a ride on a small plane to Valdez on a fact-finding mission. As she flew over the *Exxon Valdez,* she saw the tanker, now with the *Exxon Baton Rouge* alongside, through the blue haze of the oil fumes. She saw the huge, shimmering slick of freshly spilled crude and nothing else. There were no booms to contain the slick, no skimmers—nothing. As far as she could see, nothing was on the way, either.

Meanwhile, Lamb was calling the local fishers who owned boats. By 9:00 A.M. (AKST) that day, 30 boats were ready and waiting to go clean up oil. Alyeska said to wait, that it was "putting together a list of boats that can go out on the spill immediately." By noon, Leland had called Alyeska again to say that 75 boats were ready. She was told that Alyeska would call her back, but it never did.

Saving the Hatcheries

Saving the salmon hatcheries was a top priority for the fishing community of Cordova. The town's livelihood for years to come depended upon the health of the millions of baby salmon due to be released into the sound shortly after the oil spill. (Photo courtesy of Natalie Forbes/ CORBIS)

For the fishers of Cordova, the timing of the oil spill could hardly have been worse. The fishers had established salmon hatcheries, built with volunteer labor, to keep the salmon populations from dropping. Now in the hatcheries were 8 million newly hatched pink salmon called fry, and 600,000 more were hatching every day.

By early April, 117 million fry were due to be released into the sound. These fry were supposed to swim and grow in the protected sound, feeding on the plankton that blooms in the spring and summer, and then head out on a two-year, 2,000-mile (3,220-km) Pacific Ocean journey. Then, several years later, following their

keen sense of smell, the salmon would return to the waters where they were born. If the waters became toxic, both the fry—the catch for future years—and the returning salmon, which are that year's catch, would be threatened. The sound's pink salmon harvest had been worth as much as $35 million in previous years. Protecting the hatcheries was an urgent priority for Lamb and all of Cordova. They were prepared to do whatever was necessary to stop the oil. Lamb later recalled that "the anger began to build when our offers to help were totally ignored."

One fisher had this to say about the situation:

> We live day to day not knowing if we're going to be allowed to fish or not. Fishing is the only thing I'm qualified for; and fishing is a challenge. It's a certain feeling of freedom. When you've caught a lot of fish you feel just great. And I think we're capable of cleaning up the oil if they'd let us. We know our weather. We know our tides, our ocean, and our boats. When something has to be done, we do it. But now we can't do anything. Our lives are out of our hands. That's the worst thing. Exxon won't give us answers; they just let us wait around.

Over the first three days before the storm that halted the cleanup operations on March 27, the anger and frustration continued to build among the fishers as the oil slick grew and the disaster spread. Lamb, Ott, and a few others went to Valdez to try to get something done about protecting the hatcheries. They spoke to the press about the fisheries, the ecology, and the impact of the oil on the ecosystem. To the press, these fishers put a face on the damage to come.

On the night of the storm, as winds pushed the oil slick toward the hatcheries, Exxon told the fishers that the oil could no longer be stopped by mechanical means and that the company was pinning its hopes on dispersants. Lamb told Iarossi that dispersants would do little to save the hatcheries and that they had to be protected with booms. "Those hatcheries have got to be

saved. The fisheries are the most important thing. And we flat are not going to give up."

Iarossi agreed to give the fishers booms and to hire all the boats that they had waiting. When he asked how soon the boats would be available, Lamb said immediately and reached for the phone. That night, as boats streamed out of Cordova's harbor and headed for the hatcheries, the "mosquito fleet" was born. The fleet arrived just ahead of the oil.

The job was close to impossible—the first boom flown over by helicopter by Exxon was too light and flimsy and kept breaking. The fishers worked 20 hours a day for days on end. One said that in the first week he spent guarding the hatchery, he slept a total of five hours.

Meanwhile, other Cordova fishers who were not working with Lamb or Exxon did what they could on their own. Tom Copeland outfitted his boat with $5,000 worth of pumps and 5-gallon (19-l) buckets. On the first day out, his crew removed 1,500 gallons (5,680 l) of oil, and on their best day, they took 2,500 gallons (9,460 l)—a full 500 buckets. Exxon's best skimmer collected just 1,200 gallons (4,540 l) of oil in a day.

In the end, the mosquito fleet did what at first seemed impossible—it managed to save the four threatened pink salmon hatcheries from oil. However, the fishing season in Prince William Sound was officially closed, devastating the fishers financially and emotionally. Cordova became a town full of fishers who could not fish. Without fish, the canneries had to close.

Suddenly, the cooperation that had saved the hatcheries disappeared. In its place was disagreement. The state of Alaska and Exxon began hiring lawyers to defend their positions. Hundreds of attorneys worked on the case, some filing huge lawsuits, and others settling out of court. Individual attorneys who had flown into Alaska seeking business approached local citizens. Anchorage attorney Paul Davis said, "Frankly, I'm appalled at the way many of my colleagues in the legal profession are descending on this

spill like vultures." Amid the arguing, Exxon promised to compensate any fishers with valid claims for the lost season.

Some people in Cordova made money because of the spill. Boats were leased for as much as $1,000 a week, often just to wait around until they were needed. Other fishers refused to work for Exxon. They felt that taking money from this company was morally wrong—that any fisher who took money from Exxon was being bought off. Ill feelings began to divide Cordova's once tight-knit community. One fisher described "a situation where a whole lot of money was thrown around and a whole lot of people's values were turned around because of that, or they found out what their real values were; found out what their neighbor's values were.... There was a lot of sense of violation in it."

Before the Exxon Valdez *oil spill, the fish-processing plants of Cordova were full of healthy fish and shellfish caught by local fishing boats in the rich waters of Prince William Sound. (Photo courtesy of Charles E. Rotkin/CORBIS)*

Riki Ott described the feelings in Cordova throughout that summer:

> First there was all positive energy to do something—"Let's go! Let's get that oil!" When we made repeated calls to try to help and ran up against Alyeska's stone wall, our feelings turned to anger and frustration. It got real negative. Then, when the oil took off [the spill began to move and spread], Cordova hit rock bottom. That's when people were mad at everything.

There was a terrible sense of loss in Cordova, brought on by the tremendous death toll of the animals, the destruction of the pristine world that the residents all loved, and the loss of their livelihoods. That summer, so many people became angry, frustrated, and upset that the Union Hall opened a "decompression

Post-Traumatic Stress Disorder

Several years after the spill, in 1991 and 1992, researchers undertook a study in Cordova and a few other communities in the region to find out if residents had emotionally recovered from the disaster. The researchers found that many people were still suffering. Using interviews and questionnaires, the researchers learned that some people in the spill area who had depended on the environment for their food or work were suffering from post-traumatic stress disorder (PTSD).

PTSD can affect people of all ages who have survived a terrifying experience, such as a war, a rape, or a disaster. A person who suffers from PTSD constantly experiences the event again in flashbacks, memories, nightmares, or frightening thoughts and may also develop eating disorders, anxiety, and fatigue. Therapy and medication are both useful in treating the disorder.

room," where people could cool off when their tempers threatened to explode.

The wreck of the *Exxon Valdez* brought a lot of stress and hardship to this community. In the years after the spill, three out of the five fish canneries in Cordova closed. The 500-boat fishing fleet would dwindle to less than half of that. Men and women who had no way to feed their families experienced a loss of self-esteem. Some people saw their marriages and families fall apart. Young people who had expected to make fishing their livelihood saw their opportunities disappear overnight. Instead of staying in the community and having a sense of history and pride in their way of life, many were forced to leave Cordova in search of jobs in other parts of the state and country. Many in Cordova turned to alcohol or other substance abuse for comfort. Another of the mental health effects of the disaster is discussed further in the "Post-Traumatic Stress Disorder" sidebar on page 56.

CHAPTER 6

The Second Spill

The community of Valdez is similar to Cordova in size, but in other ways, Valdez is a very different place. Valdez is an oil town, a place where the motto "Home of the Supertanker" can be seen on coffee mugs and sweatshirts. Valdez is also a transportation hub linked to larger communities, such as Anchorage, by the only two-lane highway in the region. Cordova is a town identified by its fishing fleet and its citizens' strong connection to Prince William Sound. Their reliance on the land and sea determines their way of life and influences their fierce respect for their environment. (The "Naming Places" sidebar on the following page tells how Prince William Sound and Valdez were named.)

The town of Valdez, Alaska, sits at the base of mountains cradling the once pristine waters of Prince William Sound. (Photo courtesy of Associated Press)

Naming Places

In the late 1700s, explorers from Spain and England set out to find new lands in the great North American northwest. On May 12, 1778, Captain James Cook, an Englishman, discovered a beautiful sound. Since the sound was unknown to Europeans, it was not on any of their maps, so the captain drew its shape and gave it a name. He called it Sandwich Sound, after his patron, the Earl of Sandwich—but back in England, when mapmakers copied Cook's drawing, they decided to change the name. The earl (who is given credit for inventing the sandwich) was not very popular at the time, so the mapmakers renamed the sound Prince William Sound, after the current prince, William. In 1790 Don Salvador Fidalgo was exploring for the king of Spain when he sailed into a bay surrounded by steep, rocky mountains. As he drew the bay on his map, he needed to give it a name. He chose Valdez, after Antonio Valdes y Basan, an official back in Spain.

Ever since 1897, when gold was discovered in the Klondike region, Valdez has been an important gateway to the interior of Alaska. In their search for gold, the first non-Native Americans came through Valdez in a great wave. Then, when the gold supply was exhausted, most of them left, and a long, quiet period began. That quiet ended suddenly in March 1964, when the Great Alaska Earthquake shook the region for an incredibly long five minutes. The sandy ground that Valdez was built on gave way, acting more like liquid than earth. The tsunami that followed the quake wiped away homes, businesses, and people, and the village of Valdez was destroyed. The survivors rebuilt their community, but this time on bedrock 4 miles (6.4 km) from the original site.

In the 1970s, another great wave of people arrived, swelling the population of Valdez to 9,000. These people were looking not for gold but for the good wages that could be earned during the construction of 800 miles (1,290 km) of pipeline. Once again, after the work was done, most of the newcomers left. Those who remained enjoyed another period of quiet. The population stayed between 3,200 and 3,900 for most of the 1980s—but that changed in 1989. The wreck of the *Exxon Valdez* would cause the biggest population boom in the town's history.

The Population Swells

People began to arrive by the end of the very first day of the spill. Into the tiny airport flew Exxon officials, underwater divers (who came to inspect the tanker), newscasters, journalists, oil experts, and scientists. Exxon set up its field headquarters in Valdez, making it the base for the rescue and cleanup operations. By the end of the third day of the spill, as Exxon staff continued to arrive— along with animal rescue people and news teams from distant continents—the population of Valdez just about doubled. By midsummer—when the cleanup operation was at its peak—the population of Valdez soared to 11,000 or 12,000. No one knows exactly what the population was, because people were everywhere and there was no way to count them.

The road to Valdez brought a constant stream of cars with people looking for work or trucks packed with goods to sell— from tents and clothing to office supplies, cleanup equipment, and food. Suddenly, a lot of food was needed—emergency workers ate more than 200 tons (181 mt) of food a week. The flights in and out of the Valdez airport, which normally averaged 10 a day, soared to 300, even 400, a day. On one day in March, a record 687 flights came and went.

Finding a place to stay became extremely difficult. Some people rented rooms, beds, or even sheds from local residents. The churches had people sleeping on the floors. Just about any house with a couch in the living room became a bed-and-breakfast

charging $100 a day. Some people came prepared to live in their own cars or campers. Many volunteers brought their own tents and camped on the beaches and out on the islands. Cars were as hard to come by as housing. There was a waiting list for rental cars even as trucks hauling cars into town were arriving from Anchorage.

The oil slick never reached the Port of Valdez, but the arrival of thousands of people in this small town became referred to as "the second spill." According to the city manager, the invasion of people placed "incredible and almost indescribable burdens on city services. The maintenance of basic sanitation, safety, and health were the immediate problems during April. As the oil spill response unfolded...the demands on the city changed."

There was a positive side to this second spill. Many businesses thrived. The rental of beds, cars, and couches put a lot of cash in people's pockets. The motels were all full even as the rates went up. Every seat in every restaurant was taken, and long lines developed at mealtimes. Gas stations, hardware stores, and clothing stores boomed. The demand for just about everything went way

When cleanup efforts appeared to be futile, protesters arrived in Valdez to denounce Exxon's lack of responsibility and its failure to control the oil spill. (Photo courtesy of Associated Press)

up. Even everyday items such as candy and newspapers were hard to keep in stock. As Exxon poured money into the cleanup effort, the personal income in the region almost doubled. According to economist Scott Goldsmith at the University of Alaska, "From an economic point of view, it was a lovely disaster."

The Downside

There was also a negative side to all of the Exxon money. Apartment rents rose by as much as $500 per month. A local teacher who worked at the community college was evicted so that the landlord could rent her apartment to Exxon. Young couples who were about to purchase their first homes lost them to Exxon. Local businesses that could not pay the $16.69 an hour that Exxon paid lost their employees. Even the local government lost employees at a time when every department was burdened with a huge amount of additional work.

In March 1991, Attorney General Dick Thornburgh announced that Exxon would pay $900 million in cleanup costs and $100 million in environmental crime penalties to state and federal governments. (Photo courtesy of Associated Press)

The people of Valdez began to suffer from the stress of the second spill. Only weeks after the spill, the local paper ran this announcement:

> The oil spill in Prince William Sound is entirely different from other disasters. Rather than a single cataclysmic event, it is an ongoing progression of events. The "low point" of a disaster is usually much easier to identify, and therefore "turning the corner" is usually much easier. The oil spill is staying at a crisis level for an extended period.

A 24-hour crisis telephone line was set up, and calls streamed in from people suffering from anxiety and depression. Violent acts, from barroom brawls to domestic violence, increased. Mental health facilities reported an increase of cases in the region from 72 to 200 percent.

Many people in Valdez, including Mayor John Devens, had favored oil development. Oil money gave Valdez a city budget six times the size of Cordova's. In the town hall, Alyeska was often called "Uncle Al." However, after the spill, many people felt betrayed by Alyeska and Exxon's failure to protect the pristine environment. For many residents, the invasion of their hometown became more and more painful as the summer wore on. Valdez had been a place where every face was familiar, where people said hello to each other on the street, and where few people bothered to lock their front doors or cars. Now people felt that they were no longer in control of their own community—it seemed as if the oil companies were in control. As citizens became frustrated and angry, officials at Exxon and Alyeska grew fearful that someone would resort to violence. The companies hired security guards and put up fences and barricades around their facilities and offices.

As mayor, Devens had to represent the people and stand up to the oil companies. This was a difficult task for a part-time mayor (he was also president of the community college) negotiating with multibillion-dollar corporations. Devens noted, "It's insulting to me to have to go to Exxon for everything this community needs. We're experiencing a lot of social problems related to the spill—fights, depression, divorces. We asked for a counselor, but Exxon turned us down.... A community shouldn't have to come begging to a company."

Suing Exxon

By September, when Exxon declared the cleanup operation to be over, the money had stopped pouring in, and the people of Prince William Sound continued to suffer. The canneries were closed, the waters remained polluted, the shores remained oiled, and fishing remained threatened. In 1994 about 14,000 local citizens from the 25 small villages that surrounded the sound sued the Exxon Corporation for damages. One law firm represented them all in a *class-action lawsuit*. Their main attorney was Brian O'Neill. The trial lasted five months. The jury had to decide if the accident was caused by reckless behavior by either Captain Hazelwood or Exxon. The lawyers focused on Hazelwood's record of alcohol abuse. They also focused on Exxon's cost-cutting activities that left officers—who should have been on the bridge of the *Exxon Valdez* that night—too exhausted to work.

On September 16, 1994, the jury returned its verdict. Captain Hazelwood had acted in a reckless manner and was in part responsible for the spill. The jury decided that he should be fined $5,000. (In a criminal trial four years earlier, he had already been fined $50,000 and sentenced to 1,000 hours of community service.) The jury said that Exxon also had acted in a reckless manner and was also responsible for the spill. Exxon was ordered to pay $5 billion to the fishers, Alaska natives, property and business owners, and municipalities who had brought the suit. This

amount was the largest sum ever set by a jury against a corporation in history.

Exxon officials were furious—$5 billion was equal to the corporation's net profit for an entire year. They argued that Exxon had already paid $1 billion in 1991 to settle environmental crime charges and civil claims brought by the federal and state government. Exxon also cited the millions of dollars that it had spent on the *Exxon Valdez* cleanup effort. The presiding judge had the power to adjust the amount of money specified to be paid, but he chose not to because, in his own words, "With relatively small expense, Exxon could have ensured that its supertanker crew were rested and not captained by a relapsed alcohol abuser."

Exxon vowed to pursue every legal means in its power to fight the settlement in the courts—and that is just what it did. In 2004 the villages of Prince William Sound were still waiting for the money, which was still tied up in the courts.

Former Exxon Valdez captain Joseph Hazelwood was convicted of negligent discharge of oil, fined $50,000, and sentenced to 1,000 hours of community service in Alaska. In this photo, he prepares breakfast at a homeless shelter in Anchorage. (Photo courtesy of Associated Press)

CHAPTER 7

"The Day the Water Died"

The Alaskan village of Chenega Bay, populated mostly by Native Americans, suffered a different fate from Valdez. Chenega Bay lost population as a result of the spill—almost half of it.

This photo shows the fishing boat Aleut Provider *in Chenega Bay. Chenega is populated by Aleuts and other Native peoples who were unable to continue their way of life in the aftermath of the* Exxon Valdez *oil spill. (Photo courtesy of Tim Thompson/CORBIS)*

Native Suffering

Like all of the communities on Prince William Sound, Chenega Bay hugged the shoreline and could be reached only by boat or small plane. Of the 200 residents, most were Aleuts, a people who had lived along the gravel beaches of Alaska for more than 8,000 years.

The Aleuts and other Native peoples of Prince William Sound live in the modern world that is Alaska today as scientists, educators, and lawyers, and many commercial fishers. The subsistence way of living is a cherished and important part of the culture that they share. The process of hunting, fishing, and gathering foods from their environment is not about money, and it is not just about food. This way of life is about how each individual fits into the natural and spirit world.

Walter Meganack, an elder and chief from a village near Cordova, spoke for his people in describing the spill:

> When the days get longer, we get ready. Boots and boats and nets and gear are prepared for the fishing time. The winter beaches are not lonely anymore, because our children and grownups visit the beaches in the springtime and gather the abundance of the sea: the shellfish, the snails, the chitons.... It was in the early springtime. No fish yet, no snails yet. But the signs were with us. The green was starting. Some birds were flying and singing. The excitement of the season had just begun. And then we heard the news. Oil in the water—lots of oil, killing lots of water. It is too shocking to understand. Never have we thought it possible for the water to die. But it is true. We walk our beaches. And the snails and the barnacles and the chitons are falling off the rocks. Dead. Dead water.... We walk our beaches, but instead of gathering life, we gather death. Dead birds. Dead otters. Dead seaweed.

The heartbreak felt in the Native communities was the heartbreak of loss, not only of the animals that died and the purity of the environment that was destroyed, but the loss of a way of life.

A Matter of Survival

After the spill, the people of Chenega Bay could not live as their ancestors had—they could not gather the natural food from the environment. The clams, mussels, and snails that were gathered by the young and elderly along the beaches were now all dead. People found dead deer with oiled kelp in their mouths. The fish were all exposed to oil, as were the crabs, mussels, shrimp, and seals. Almost all the traditional foods such as these were poisoned. Once the shores around Chenega Bay were coated in oil, the people had to go to nontraditional communities in order to work for wages to buy packaged food.

Some Native communities unaffected by the spill collected traditional foods and flew them to the people of Prince William Sound in a program called the Native to Native Assistance Program. Exxon also sent food, but it was store-bought food, like chicken. Many of the Native people consider store-bought food less healthy and less tasty than the natural food from their environment. Many refused to eat the "Exxon chicken," as it was called by the children. Others just lost their appetites and became depressed.

Native people knew that they had to make enough money to purchase food through the next winter. Usually, they dried and smoked fish and meats for winter, but that was not possible this year. Many men and women got jobs cleaning beaches for Exxon; in some families, both parents took these jobs. Cleaning beaches meant putting in long hours—often, it meant returning home at midnight and leaving for work again at dawn. Children left at home became fearful. The forests and beaches where they once had played were littered with dead eagles, murres, and otters. Many of the children began to suffer from nightmares.

On the job, some Natives ran into racism because other people felt that the Natives were not smart or sophisticated enough to offer solutions. Other Natives were frustrated by the show that Exxon and its contractors put on for the press. Marvin Fox, Jr. was a young worker on a beach cleanup crew when a group of journalists were flown in to see the beach after it was "cleaned" with pressurized hoses. The reporters were impressed until Fox pushed the nozzle of his pressurized hose into the gravel, causing black oil to ooze up. His uncle described what happened next: "After those reporters left, a...foreman shoved the kid. They grabbed him, twisted his arm, and said, 'What the hell do you think you're doing? You're fired!'"

An abandoned cannery in Chenega Harbor illustrates how hard the village was hit by the Exxon Valdez oil spill. Fishing, the town's only industry, was destroyed by the disaster. (Photo courtesy of Roy Corral/CORBIS)

Native people were also frustrated by the apparent futility of the cleanup, which seemed to never end. According to Chief Meganack,

> The oil companies lied about preventing a spill. Now they lie about the cleanup. Our people know what happens on the beaches. Spend all day cleaning one big rock, and the tide comes in and covers it with oil again. Spend a week wiping and spraying the surface, but pick up a rock and there's 4 inches [10.2 cm] of oil underneath.

A wave of reporters invaded the Native communities of Prince William Sound in the wake of the oil spill. Boatloads of reporters came from New York City, California, and as far away as Japan and Australia. They took pictures of the elders, the children, the houses and gardens. If they were not invited into people's homes, they tried to take pictures through the windows. They were trying to put a human face on the tragedy of the spill, but they became as hated as Exxon. One young man said that living with so many

The rocky coastline of Chenega Bay was covered in oil. Even after beaches and coastline were cleaned, oil that had seeped into the ground oozed up to coat the surface again. (Photo courtesy of National Oceanic and Atmospheric Administration)

strangers around changed the community: "It was like living in an apartment and then all of a sudden there are ten people that you don't know who come in and live with you."

People had to lock their doors—something that they had never done before. In one village, the local leaders issued a ban on travel into the village. When a plane approached for landing, it was radioed and told that "if there are any reporters on the plane, don't think about landing. They are not welcome here." In Chenega, someone looked out the window to see a man landing in the garden with a parachute!

When the summer came to a close, the reporters left and the cleanup operation ended. The good jobs also ended. Many people left Chenega to work in non-Native communities and send food home by plane through the long Alaskan winter. These young men and women could no longer live the traditional way, but they helped Chenega Bay survive.

CHAPTER 8

The Legacy

In this photo, workers transport birds covered in oil to a rehabilitation center for cleaning and eventual release into cleaner waters. (Photo courtesy of Gary Braasch/CORBIS)

Before 1989, environmentalists had been saying that better laws were needed to protect U.S. soil and waters from oil spills. As Americans watched the disaster in Prince William Sound unfold, they began to agree. Many called their representatives in Congress, demanding that the government do something. In the nation's capital, members of Congress scrambled to look at the laws that were already on the books, analyze where they fell short, and propose solutions. At the time of the *Exxon Valdez* spill,

there was vigorous debate in Congress about the effectiveness of double-hulled tankers. (A double-hulled tanker has two hulls to prevent liquid cargo from spilling in an accident. If the outer hull is damaged, the inner hull keeps the cargo in place.) In addition, lawmakers realized that the federal government did not have any specific plans to divert emergency money and resources in the event of a disastrous oil spill. The solutions that they proposed were written into the Oil Pollution Act (OPA) of 1990.

With the passage of the law, all new tankers entering Prince William Sound have to be constructed with double hulls. Tankers already in service—single-hulled tankers—have to be modified with double hulls or taken out of service by the year 2015. A double hull would have greatly lessened the amount of the oil spilled from the *Exxon Valdez*.

The OPA also includes stricter regulations for tankers while they are berthed. Booms are now required around a tanker in order to contain any oil that might spill during the difficult loading (or offloading) operation. As a supertanker loads up with oil, a team inspects the tanker and oil hoses hourly, checking for leaks or spills. The act also toughens the licensing of tanker personnel regarding drug or alcohol abuse. As the ship is readied to depart, the captain, and sometimes the crew, is tested for alcohol use.

If this story were reenacted today, the tanker could not be the *Exxon Valdez*—it was barred from Prince William Sound by the OPA in a ruling that prohibits any tanker that has spilled more than 1 million gallons (3.8 million l) from entering the sound. (Its fate is discussed in "The *Exxon Valdez* Today" sidebar on page 74.) The captain of the ship could not be Captain Hazelwood. He was fired.

Today, a well-equipped, 210-foot (64-m) Escort Response Vessel (ERV) and a strong, oceangoing tugboat accompany any tanker that leaves the terminal until it exits the sound and enters the Pacific Ocean. ERVs are equipped with hoses and pumps that can retrieve oil from the surface of seawater in the event of a leak or spill. The Coast Guard tracks the ship's location with upgraded

The *Exxon Valdez* Today

By April 5, 1989, the lightering of the *Exxon Valdez* was complete, and the tanker was towed to a nearby island for temporary repairs. On June 23, the ship was seaworthy enough to be escorted to a shipyard in San Diego, California, where repairs were completed. The *Exxon Valdez* was still one of the best ships in the Exxon fleet, but wherever it went, its name would be recognized. Around the world, the name *Exxon Valdez* had become synonymous with the term *oil spill,* so Exxon officials renamed the ship *Exxon Mediterranean.* Later, it became the *SeaRiver Mediterranean.* Barred from Prince William Sound by law, the tanker delivers Middle Eastern crude oil to European ports. But the tanker is really too large for that route. This ship was built for the Valdez-to-California run. Exxon has applied to have the law that bars the tanker from Alaska reversed, but citizens continue to protest its return, no matter what the ship is now called. The courts have refused to reverse the law.

equipment. When there is ice in the channel, one of the escort boats serves as a scout, using large searchlights, if necessary.

As the tanker nears the place where the *Exxon Valdez* ran aground, a lighted beacon can be seen shining from the reef. Now, it is not until the tanker has safely passed Bligh Reef that the harbor pilot leaves the tanker and returns to Valdez.

Who Is Responsible?

The OPA also resolves the confusion over who is in charge of a cleanup operation. According to the OPA, a committee of people from the local community, headed by an on-site federal officer, would become command central. If a spill occurred in a navigable waterway, the U.S. Coast Guard would certify the committee and manage the cleanup operation. If the spill occurred on U.S. soil, the EPA would be responsible. The committees would be part of a nationwide system under the National Response Plan (NRP). The NRP's system includes 22 regional spill-response sites around the contiguous states, Alaska, Hawaii, and the Caribbean. At these sites, equipment—including booms, skimmers, and dispersants—is available. The system also includes a national response center where the location and availability of spill-response equipment and personnel are listed on computers. If 400 yards (366 m) of fireproof boom heavy enough for choppy water conditions is suddenly needed, the computer database can give the exact location and quantity available of that item.

The OPA makes the oil companies, or spillers, physically and financially responsible for the cleanup. By law, oil companies are now required to have specially trained spill-response personnel standing by 24 hours a day, 7 days a week. In Prince William

One legacy of the Exxon Valdez *oil spill is increased funds to enforce new, stricter regulations for oil tankers and the transfer of oil in American waters. In this photo, U.S. Coast Guard seamen control traffic and monitor rescue boats and weather conditions at the Coast Guard vessel traffic center in Seattle, Washington. (Photo courtesy of Associated Press)*

Sound, the *Ship Escort and Response Vessel Service* (SERVS) vessel is now always present and ready. In the event of a spill, this new high-tech ship will start retrieving oil from the water surface immediately. With a staff of 250 specially trained men and women, SERVS is one of the best oil-spill prevention and response forces in the world.

The Sound Slowly Recovers

Many other things have changed since that night in 1989 when the *Exxon Valdez* departed for points south, laden with North Slope crude. Out in the water, sea otters still float on their backs in the kelp beds, but there are fewer of them. The sea otter population has yet to reach the numbers recorded before the spill. The kelp beds that form such an important part of their habitat have not yet recovered, either. They were killed by the beach-cleaning activities. With the dying of the kelp beds, all the marine life that found shelter and food in them suffered.

In 1992 the herring returned to spawn, but they were sick and covered with lesions. The cause is unknown, but the oil pollution was at least part of it. Herring are a very important part of the food chain of the sound—just about everything eats herring. They are one of the favorite foods of the beautiful, silvery harbor seals. The seal population was already falling before the spill. After the spill, harbor seal pups born on oiled beaches died, and the population fell sharply.

Today, fewer birds fly out over the water. The common murre, cormorant, harlequin duck, and common loon are some of the species that have not reproduced in numbers large enough to match their former populations. There is no empirical evidence as to why this is, though it seems likely that the oil pollution affected reproduction rates. Along the shores, the clams and mussels have yet to recover completely. Biologists estimate that the animal population of the sound may recover in 20 to 70 years. The eagles are

one of the only success stories. There are more eagle pairs today than there were on that spring day in March 1989.

The Native population of Valdez and surrounding villages is also trying to return to the way of life they knew before the disaster. Aleuts continue to mend their nets and to fish, hunt, and gather food from their environment as their ancestors did. However, they worry that the food is polluted. Many Aleuts have left their homes on the bay to live in nontraditional communities and work in nontraditional jobs.

Some of the fishers of Cordova still look forward to the opening of the fishing season each spring, but others have given up fishing and declared bankruptcy. Four years after the spill, Cordova went from being the 9th-leading port in the nation for commercial fish harvest to the 51st. The town's fleet of fishing boats is just over half of what it once was. Many couples that bought boat and fishing licenses for $300,000, as an investment

Tragic images of struggling wildlife poisoned by the oil spilled from the Exxon Valdez *serve as a grave reminder of the damage done to one of the most pristine regions of the United States. (Photo courtesy of Roy Corral/CORBIS)*

that could be passed on to their children, have had to sell the licenses for less than $50,000.

During the *Exxon Valdez* crisis, many people across the nation and around the world who saw Prince William Sound on the news wanted to see the beauty of the place for themselves. Now, on any warm summer afternoon, the streets of Valdez are

Even as new and cleaner forms of energy are being utilized, environmentalists are working to prevent more damage to wildlife. In 1998 an environmental impact report called for the replacement of these windmills in Livermore, California, with newer models designed to spare birds that were being killed by the hundreds. (Photo courtesy of Associated Press)

crowded with tourists. Today, Valdez is home of the cruise ship, as well as the supertanker.

What happened to the oil? There are many different theories and estimates. Eventually, between 15 and 40 percent of the spill evaporated into the atmosphere. About 15,000 gallons (56,760 l) were burned. About 58 percent washed up onto the beaches. Exxon's cleanup effort recovered between 8 and 23 percent. The rest of the oil remains on the seafloor, under the rocky beaches, and in organisms. The mousse that remained in the water eventually hardened into tar balls and sank to the bottom. These tar balls continue to wash up onto the beaches today.

New Oil Awareness?

The legacy of the *Exxon Valdez* goes beyond the OPA. After the disaster, many Americans questioned their country's—and even their own—dependency on oil. As a citizen of Valdez said, "It's not just the oil companies, it's all of us that caused this disaster." This growing awareness on the part of Americans led to research on improved appliance efficiency standards, more fuel-efficient cars, and new energy-saving building codes. Americans started demanding alternative sources of energy, such as wind power and solar power. But today, Americans still use more oil than any other people on Earth—about 16.2 million barrels a day—and the demand for oil continues to rise.

CHAPTER 9

Conclusion

In a world that uses 3 billion gallons (11 billion l) of oil a day, oil spills have become part of life. Environmentalists around the world have pushed for lessening our dependence on oil, but scientists have identified at least 500,000 different uses for oil, from fuel to spandex to artificial turf. Since people in the 21st century depend on oil, scientists are looking for ways to lessen the cost to the environment and to help the victims of future spills.

This worker is monitoring a beach in Prince William Sound to assess how far up the beach the oil reaches and how effective the tide is in washing away the poisonous sludge. (Photo courtesy of National Oceanic and Atmospheric Administration)

As soon as the news spread that 11 million gallons (41.6 million l) of oil had entered the Prince William Sound ecosystem, scientists flocked to the region. Biologists, zoologists, economists, sociologists, environmentalists, chemists, and cleanup experts came to observe, measure, and analyze the impact of the disaster on all the organisms of the sound, from the people in their communities to the algae in the water.

One group of scientists who examined the impact of the oil spill in Prince William Sound was sociologists who study disasters. Steve Picou, a professor at the University of South Alabama, studied different disasters and their impact on people. Six years after the spill, Picou found that 40 percent of the men in Cordova, mostly fishers, were still suffering from severe depression. They felt that their community had been torn apart. Picou has found that human-made disasters often do tear communities apart. When a human-made disaster hits, the first question asked is who is to blame, and lawyers are among the first people to arrive.

When a community is struck by an earthquake or hurricane, everyone bands together to protect the residents and rebuild the community. The first people on the scene are from the Red Cross. There are no questions about who is to blame. Natural disasters tend to bring communities together.

When a natural disaster strikes, the damage may be enormous, but the worst is quickly over. Human-made environmental disasters, however, continue over a long period of time, year after year. They often pollute things that cannot be repaired quickly—the water, air, and soil. They begin to feel like disasters in slow motion. And the people who caused the disaster are often the ones that communities have to work with to clean it up, just as the men and women of Prince William Sound had to go to Exxon for help in protecting the hatcheries and cleaning the beaches. As Chief Meganack put it: "We fight a rich and powerful giant, the oil industry, while at the same time we take orders and a paycheck from it. We are torn in half." Bill Freudenburg, a sociologist from the University of Wisconsin who also studies disasters, says that "it's like putting Hurricane Opal in charge of cleaning up Florida. There's something funny about that."

Exxon made a huge effort to fix the damage done. The cost of the cleanup and rescue operations was $2 billion. The company paid out $300 million to fishers and Native Americans for the loss of the 1989 fishing season. Exxon also paid $100 million in a criminal fine to the government and another $900 million to restoration projects over a 10-year period. A lot of good things were done with this money, but in the end, money did not, and could not, fix the disaster. Prince William Sound will have to heal itself in time—and the people will have to heal each other. In the words of Chief Walter Meganack, "I am an elder. I am chief. I will not lose hope. We have never before lived through this kind of death. But we have lived through lots of other kinds of death. We will learn from the past, we will learn from each other, and we will live. Where there is life there is hope."

Time Line

1975

March   Construction of the Trans-Alaska Pipeline begins

1977

June   Construction of the Trans-Alaska Pipeline is completed

June 20   North Slope oil begins to flow through the pipeline to Valdez, Alaska

August 1   The *ARCO Juneau*, the first tanker laden with North Slope crude, leaves Valdez

Photo courtesy of Associated Press

1989

March 24, 12:04 A.M. (AKST)   The *Exxon Valdez* runs aground on Bligh Reef

March 24, 12:26 A.M. (AKST)   Captain Hazelwood calls the Valdez Traffic Center (VTC) to report that the *Exxon Valdez* has run aground and is leaking oil

March 24, 12:30 A.M. (AKST)   The Coast Guard notifies Alyeska of the oil spill

March 24, 4:14 A.M. (AKST)   The *Exxon Baton Rouge* is directed to proceed to the *Exxon Valdez* to begin lightering operations

March 24, 12:40 P.M. (AKST)   Alyeska's barge with cleanup equipment arrives at the site of the spill

March 24, 6:00 P.M. (AKST)   Dispersants are tried to break up the oil slick, but are ineffective

March 25, 7:36 A.M. (AKST)   The lightering of the *Exxon Valdez* begins

March 25, 12:00 P.M. (AKST)	Exxon officially takes over responsibility for the cleanup, relieving Alyeska
March 25, 4:00 P.M. (AKST)	Another dispersant test proves unsuccessful
March 25, 8:45 P.M. (AKST)	About 15,000 gallons (56,760 l) of oil are burned in a test
March 26, 11:00 A.M. (AKST)	Another dispersant test proves unsuccessful
March 26, 2:30 P.M. (AKST)	The first successful dispersant test is made in choppy waters
March 26, 3:00 P.M. (AKST)	The Alaska National Guard is activated to help with the cleanup
March 26, 5:00 P.M. (AKST)	The use of dispersants is approved for one area of the spill
March 26, 6:30 P.M. (AKST)	Alaska governor Steve Cowper declares a state of emergency
March 26, 9:00 P.M. (AKST)	A burning operation planned for the next morning is canceled due to high winds

March 27, 6:00 A.M. (AKST)	Storm winds blow up to 73 miles (117 km) an hour during the early morning hours, ruining the day's cleanup plans
March 27, 1:30 P.M. (AKST)	Exxon is told that beach cleanup crews will be needed; oil is reported 37 miles (59.5 km) from the site of the spill
March 28, 1:30 P.M. (AKST)	A mousse-burning operation proves unsuccessful
March 28, 2:00 P.M. (AKST)	Oil is reported 52 miles (84 km) from the site of the spill
March 29, 8:00 A.M. (AKST)	Beach cleaning operations begin; Exxon reports that a total of 5,000 to 6,000 barrels of oil have been recovered mechanically
March 30	Oil is reported 90 miles (145 km) from the site of the spill

April 2	Exxon reports that a total of 10,000 barrels of oil have been recovered mechanically
April 3	Oil is reported 140 miles (225 km) from the site of the spill
April 5	The *Exxon Valdez* is floated off Bligh Reef and towed to a nearby island for emergency repairs
April 7	Oil is reported 180 miles (290 km) from the site of the spill
April 14	Oil is reported 250 miles (400 km) from the site of the spill
May 2	Oil is reported 350 miles (560 km) from the site of the spill
May 18	Oil is reported 470 miles (760 km) from the site of the spill
June 23	The *Exxon Valdez* leaves Prince William Sound and is towed to San Diego, California, for repairs
September 15	The Exxon cleanup operation officially comes to an end

Photo courtesy of Associated Press

1990

August	Congress passes the Oil Pollution Act (OPA)

1991

October 9	Exxon settles with the state of Alaska and the U.S. government, agreeing to pay $1 billion in penalties

1994

September 16	Exxon is ordered to pay a settlement of $5 billion in a class-action lawsuit; Exxon officials vow to fight the decision in court

Chronology of Oil Spills

The following list is a selection of major oil spills of the last 40 years.

1967

March 18

Torrey Canyon

Cornwall, England

38.2 million gallons
    (144.5 million l) spilled

1972

December 19

Sea Star

Gulf of Oman

37.9 million gallons
    (143.4 million l) spilled

1975

January

Jakob Maersk

Oporto, Portugal

24.3 million gallons
    (92 million l) spilled

1977

February 25

Hawaiian Patriot

Hawaiian Islands

31.2 million gallons
    (118.1 million l) spilled

1978

March 16

Amoco Cadiz

Portsall, France

68 million gallons
    (257 million l) spilled

1979

March

Independenta

Bosporus, Turkey

28.9 million gallons
    (109.4 million l) spilled

July 19

Atlantic Empress

Tobago, West Indies

43 million gallons
    (163 million l) spilled

1980

February

Irenes Serenade

Navarino Bay, Greece

36.6 million gallons
   (138.5 million l) spilled

1983

August 6

Castillo de Bellver

Cape Town, South Africa

78.5 million gallons
   (297 million l) spilled

1984

November

MV Puerto Rican

San Francisco, California,
   United States

1.5 million gallons
   (5.7 million l) spilled

1988

November

Odyssey

Newfoundland, Canada

43.1 million gallons
   (163.1 million l) spilled

1989

March 24

Exxon Valdez

Valdez, Alaska, United States

11 million gallons
   (41.6 million l) spilled

December 19

Khark 5

Oualidia, Morocco

20 million gallons
   (75.7 million l) spilled

1990

February 7

American Trader

Bosa Chica, California,
   United States

300,000 gallons (1.1 million l)
   spilled

1991

April

Haven

Genoa, Italy

42 million gallons
   (159 million l) spilled

May 28

ABT Summer

Angola

15 million gallons
   (56.8 million l) spilled

1992

December 3

Aegean Sea

La Coruna, Spain

21 million gallons
    (79.5 million l) spilled

Katina P.

South Africa

15 million gallons
    (56.8 million l) spilled

1993

January 5

Braer

Shetland Islands, Scotland

25 million gallons
    (94.6 million l) spilled

1994

March 31

Seki

Fujairah, United Arab Emirates

4 million gallons (15.1 million l)
    spilled

1996

February 15

Sea Empress

Milford Haven, Wales

21 million gallons (79 million l)
    spilled

1999

December 12

Erika

France

3 million gallons (11.4 million l)
    spilled

2000

January 4

Volganeft 248

Istanbul, Turkey

260,000 gallons (983,800 l)
    spilled

October 4

Natuna Sea

Batu Berhanti, Indonesia

2 million gallons (7.6 million l)
    spilled

November 28

Westchester

New Orleans, Louisiana,
    United States

567,000 gallons (2.1 million l)
    spilled

2002

January 22

Eastern Fortitude

Rayong Bay, Thailand

26,400 gallons (100,000 l)
    spilled

Photo courtesy of Associated Press

Glossary

Alyeska A consortium of oil companies that built, owned, and operated the Trans-Alaska Pipeline and terminal facilities

bioremediation The use of microorganisms to break down toxic pollutants in the environment, such as spilled oil

booms Long, flexible, plastic tubes used to contain an oil slick on water

bridge A raised structure on a ship, from which the ship is controlled

class-action lawsuit A lawsuit brought by one person on behalf of others who have been injured

consortium A partnership of two or more businesses in a common venture

crash stop The procedure by which a tanker moving at "full ahead" comes to a stop

crude oil Oil that has not been treated for usage

dispersants Chemicals or solvents that break down an oil slick into tiny droplets that quickly sink down into the water

dissolution Dissolving or breaking into parts

ecosystem A community of plants, animals, and other organisms that interact with each other and the environment that they live in

Environmental Protection Agency (EPA) A U.S. agency responsible for protecting the natural environment

evaporation   The process by which a liquid converts to vapor

helmsman   The person who steers a ship

hypothermia   The condition of having a body temperature below normal

intertidal zone   The area between the high tide and low tide marks along a shore

lightering   The process of moving oil from one tanker to another

loon   A type of seabird

mousse   A mixture of water, crude oil, and oxygen

murre   A type of seabird

oil field   A region rich in oil deposits, usually containing working oil wells

oil refinery   A factory where crude oil is processed into fuel for various usages

oil slick   A layer of oil floating on the surface of water

otter   A type of marine mammal

pipeline   A line of pipes used to transport oil

reef   A mass of rock or coral that rises up to or near the surface of a body of water

Ship Escort and Response Vessel Service (SERVS)   An oil-spill prevention and response force on Prince William Sound

skimmers   Boats that suck up or skim oil from the surface of water

sound   A long, wide, protected inlet of the ocean

stern   The rear of a ship

supersucker   A large vacuum truck built to clean up oil spills

supertanker   An extremely large ship, with a capacity of over 100,000 tons (91,000 mt), that has large tanks in the hull for carrying oil or other liquids

tsunami   Japanese for "harbor wave"; a great wave resulting from shock waves created by an earthquake

Ultra Large Crude Carrier (ULCC)   A supertanker that can carry over 500,000 tons (454,000 mt)

Very Large Crude Carrier (VLCC)   A supertanker that can carry between 100,000 and 500,000 tons (91,000 and 454,000 mt)

weathering   The process by which a substance breaks down into its parts due to exposure to air, wind, waves, sunlight, and microorganisms

Further Reading and Web Sites

Alaska SeaLife Center. A facility that helps to maintain Alaska's marine ecosystem. Available online. URL: http://www.alaskasealife.org/. Accessed August 6, 2004.

Alyeska Pipeline Service Company. The home page for Alyeska and the Trans-Alaska Pipeline System. Available online. URL: http://www.alyeska-pipe.com/. Accessed August 6, 2004.

American Geological Institute (AGI). This web site provides information on geology and tries to increase public awareness of the important role that geological science plays in the use of natural resources and interaction with the environment. Available online. URL: http://www.agiweb.org. Accessed November 10, 2004.

Anchorage Daily News. The web site for this Alaska newspaper has many fascinating, up-to-date articles about Alaska. Available online. URL: http://www.adn.com/. Accessed August 6, 2004.

Berger, Melvin. *Oil Spill!* New York: HarperCollins, 1994. This book explains what causes oil spills to occur and discusses how they can be prevented.

Black, Wallace B., and Jean F. Blashfield. *Oil Spills* (Saving Planet Series). Markham, Ontario, Canada: Scholastic Library Publishing, 1991. This book discusses several environmental disasters involving oil spills. The book provides information on the toxicity of oil to plants and animals, cleanup techniques, and methods of preventing oil spill accidents in the future.

Bryan, Nichol. Exxon Valdez: *Oil Spill* (Environmental Disasters). Cleveland: World Almanac Library, 2003. A well-illustrated introduction to the *Exxon Valdez* oil spill disaster with a conclusion discussing alternatives to oil for fuel.

Carr, Terry. *Spill! The Story of the* Exxon Valdez. New York: Franklin Watts, 1991. A nonpolitical report on the disaster, the events leading up to it, and its consequences, based on firsthand accounts.

Davidson, Art. *In the Wake of the* Exxon Valdez: *The Devastating Impact of the Alaska Oil Spill.* San Francisco: Sierra Club Books, 1990. The story of the disaster and the tragic consequences for the environment—uses dozens of eyewitness accounts.

Dils, Tracey E. *The* Exxon Valdez. Philadelphia: Chelsea House, 2001. The story of the oil spill, the environmental damage, and the reforms resulting from the disaster.

Environmental News Network (ENN). This web site offers viewers timely environmental news reports. The goal of the organization is to educate the public about major environmental issues, including actions that people can take in their own communities. Available online. URL: http://www.enn.com/. Accessed November 10, 2004.

Exxon Valdez Oil Spill Trustee Council. This organization monitors the restoration of the ecosystem that was damaged by the *Exxon Valdez* oil spill. Available online. URL: http://www.evostc.state.ak.us/. Accessed August 6, 2004.

Infoplease—Oil Spills. An encyclopedic web site offering a detailed chronology of oil spills around the world from 1976 to the present. Available online. URL: http://www.infoplease.com/ipa/A0001451.html. Accessed August 6, 2004.

International Bird Rescue Research Center (IBRRC). Center dedicated to reducing the human effect on birds and wildlife around the world. Available online. URL: http://www.ibrrc.org/. Accessed August 6, 2004.

International Tanker Owners Pollution Federation (ITOPF) Limited—Fate & Effects: Effects of Marine Oil Spills. A nonprofit organization offers technical information and services for responding to oil spills. Available online. URL: http://www.itopf.com/effects.html. Accessed August 6, 2004.

Keeble, John. *Out of the Channel: The* Exxon Valdez *Oil Spill in Prince William Sound.* New York: HarperCollins, 1991. Interviews of witnesses combined with a tale of money and litigation, as well as an account of the civil suit following the disaster.

Lampton, Christopher. *Oil Spill.* Brookfield, Conn.: Millbrook Press, 1992. Relates the causes of oil spills, as well as their impact on the environment and methods of cleaning them up.

Margulies, Phillip. Exxon Valdez *Oil Spill* (When Disaster Strikes! Series). New York: Rosen Publishing Group, 2003. Tells of the factors leading up to the spill, the response to the disaster, and the lasting consequences.

Markle, Sandra. *After the Spill: The* Exxon Valdez, *Then and Now.* New York: Walker, 1999. A photo essay about the spill, its effect on the environment and residents of Prince William Sound, and the action that was taken to prevent a similar disaster.

Planet Ark. A web site offering daily news and information on environmental issues around the world. Available online. URL: http://www.planetark.com. Accessed August 6, 2004.

Prince William Sound: An Ecosystem in Transition. A National Oceanic and Atmospheric Administration (NOAA) web site that examines the effects of the *Exxon Valdez* oil spill on Prince William Sound. Available online. URL: http://www.response.restoration.noaa.gov/bat/about.html. Accessed August 6, 2004.

Prince William Sound Science Center. This independent research center located in Cordova, Alaska, studies the regional ecology. Available online. URL: http://www.pwssc.gen.ak.us/. Accessed August 6, 2004.

Pringle, Laurence. *Oil Spills: Damage, Recovery, and Prevention.* New York: Morrow Junior Books, 1993. Details the uses of oil, the impact of a spill, and ways to prevent and clean up a spill.

Sherrow, Victoria. *The* Exxon Valdez: *Tragic Oil Spill.* Springfield, N.J.: Enslow, 1998. An account of the grounding of the supertanker, reasons for the accident, and possible lessons learned from the disaster.

Spencer, Page. *White Silk and Black Tar: A Journal of the Alaska Oil Spill.* Minneapolis: Bergamot, 1990. A personal account of the tragic disaster by an ecologist and Native Alaskan.

Streissguth, Thomas, and Gil Chandler. *The* Exxon Valdez: *The Oil Spill off the Alaskan Coast* (Disaster!). Mankato, Minn.: Capstone High-Interest Books, January 2002. A retelling of the disaster and its aftereffects.

ThinkQuest—Prince William Sound: Paradise Lost? An online library web site offering a report that summarizes the *Exxon Valdez* disaster, including history, cleanup, and results. Available online. URL: http://library.thinkquest.org/ 10867/home.shtml. Accessed August 6, 2004.

U.S. Environmental Protection Agency (EPA) Oil Program— *Exxon Valdez.* This page is from the official web site of the government agency that monitors the U.S. environment. Includes an extensive history on the *Exxon Valdez* oil spill and information on preventing and responding to oil spills in general. Available online. URL: http://www.epa.gov/ oilspill/exxon.htm. Accessed August 6, 2004.

Wheelwright, Jeff. *Degrees of Disasters: Prince William Sound: How Nature Reels and Rebounds.* New Haven, Conn.: Yale University Press, 1996. A review of the effects that the *Exxon Valdez* oil spill had on the environment. The author argues that the cleanup efforts did more harm than good and that nature would have repaired itself in a more efficient way.

Index